LISE KRISTENSEN was born as Lisena Onona Nielsen in Java, Indonesia, in 1954 to Norwegian parents. During the Second World War, she and her family were held for over two years in Japanese prisoner-of-war camps on the island. After the war they moved to Norway.

She is now a painter, and exhibits and sells her work in Europe, the USA and Japan. She lives in Spain with her husband.

Please return/renew this item by the last date shown on this label, or on your self-service receipt.

To renew this item, visit **www.librarieswest.org.uk** or contact your library.

Your Borrower number and PIN are required.

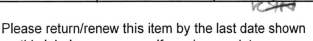

LibrariesWest

The Little Captive

Lise Kristensen

PAN BOOKS

First published 2012 as *The Blue Door* by Macmillan

First published in paperback 2014 as *The Little Captive* by Pan Books
an imprint of Pan Macmillan, a division of Macmillan Publishers Limited
Pan Macmillan, 20 New Wharf Road, London N1 9RR
Basingstoke and Oxford
Associated companies throughout the world
www.panmacmillan.com

ISBN 978-1-4472-7356-1

1 3 5 7 9 8 6 4 2

A CIP catalogue record for this book is available from the British Library.

Printed and bound by CPI Group (UK) Ltd, Croydon, CR0 4YY

Visit **www.panmacmillan.com** to read more about all our books
and to buy them. You will also find features, author interviews and
news of any author events, and you can sign up for e-newsletters
so that you're always first to hear about our new releases.

To my brave mother

Contents

CHAPTER I

War in Asia

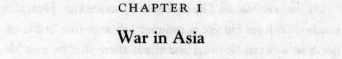

1942

It was towards the middle of the year when my friends started disappearing. I was so looking forward to going back to school, but our teacher, Miss Overhaart, and others, too, had disappeared. When I went to look for my friend Elly, I found a Javanese family living in her house. The man was nasty and didn't smile when he opened the door. He said that Elly's family had been locked up in prison, but that was a lie because Elly's family were kind and were not criminals, so why would they be locked up in prison?

I remember listening in on a conversation between two of Papa's friends, and they talked about a man called Hitler who wanted to control the world. A little later I asked Mama about this man Hitler, but she said little girls shouldn't worry about such a nasty person. Besides, this was Indonesia, and all the nastiness was happening on the other side of the world.

It hadn't impacted on my happy existence on Java. I had lived there all my life, but both my parents were from Bergen, Norway.

My father, Daniel Grønn-Nielsen, moved to Java after he finished college. He got a summer job as a tour guide on the fjords in western Norway, and it was there that he met Mr and Mrs Verhoog – Dutch people who were living in Indonesia and holidaying in Norway.

Mr Verhoog was Governor in Madiun, and thought there would be suitable employment for Papa in Java. Our mother, Kirsten, was engaged to father and followed him a year later. They were married with a grand reception at the Verhoog family residence.

The Governor also had several guest residences, and our family often lived in one of these for weeks at a time. Life was very good. I was born in Surabaya in 1934. My sister, Karin, was born in Kediri in 1936.

Papa travelled extensively around most of Java, from Batavia (Jakarta) to Surabaya, in his job as an insurance and security representative for a Dutch-American company, so he was seldom at home. Sometimes he stayed for longer on a particular job, and his family were then allocated a house.

Mama had a good life after we were born. We had lots of servants, among them a childminder, or baboe, and we would speak Javanese to the servants, but Dutch to our parents and friends. We only spoke Norwegian on Wednesdays – Mama called it Norwegian Day – when we ate typical Norwegian food like meatballs, boiled potatoes and pea soup. It was very unlike the delicious Indonesian food we were used to, the spicy dried meat, eggs, fish and chicken in curry and paprika-onion sauce – and fried bananas. We tried very hard to learn to speak Norwegian but it was not easy.

There was always plenty for me and my sister to do as we grew up with Mr and Mrs Verhoog, who became our adoptive grandparents: 'Oma' and 'Opa'. They had a huge fish pond in the grounds and all kinds of dogs, birds, geese and several peacocks. Opa was also a keen orchid specialist, and I loved being in his nursery tending the flowers and listening to the stories of all the different species he had been able to grow. Of course there were swimming pools close by, where Mama and Papa, with their friends and children, always had a great time when the heat got unbearable. Java is only three degrees south of the Equator.

It was always so exciting at the swimming pools. Our handsome Papa would dive from the high boards like a true professional and impress the ladies, who would shout, 'Da capo! Da capo!' Karin and I were so proud; this was our Papa! Only Mama looked bored and sad as the ladies sat themselves ever closer to him. 'One or two of the ladies are his secretaries,' Mama whispered one day. I noticed that they were very beautiful. 'Now look at me, fat and pregnant.' She sighed. I did not know what to say, as she was very unhappy at the time and argued a lot with Papa.

Many afternoons Mama took us horseback riding in the rice fields. We rented three horses, two small and one big, and two natives guided us. We rode out to the *kampongs* (small

3

Indonesian villages) where women stood in murky water up to their knees planting rice – small sprigs that they pushed down into the mud. Between the fields were passages that the horses could walk on. Close to the *kampongs* they had small 'factories' where they produced bricks. Children as young as six mixed clay and sand to push into wooden boxes. They left them to dry, then removed the bricks from the boxes and burned them in large ovens. I felt so sorry for them and wanted to give them something, but Mama said that if we did, the grown-ups would take it from them.

Other children were stuck behind huge looms, working like grown-ups, just like the ones behind the large ploughs pulled by oxen. None of these children went to school. I remember the Javanese children of the employees at the Dutch rubber and coffee plantations all wearing uniforms when they went to their multi-lingual school.

My parents' best friends were Uncle Axel and Aunt Marianne Wieslander. They weren't my real uncle and aunt, but they were just like family. They were Swedish and Mama said that Sweden wasn't in the war so they were safe from the Japanese. Uncle Axel had changed: he no longer laughed and joked with us like he used to; now he was serious all the time. One day, when he came to our house, he offered Papa a job doing the finance in his factory. Uncle Axel was very important: not only was he the Swedish Consul, he was director of the factory that made ball bearings, SKF (Svenska Kullagerfabriken). He told

Papa that if he took a job with him we would be safe from the Japanese.

But my friends were not safe. One by one those from the Dutch community simply vanished. In addition to Elly and her brother Cees, Renee, Erika and Ina all disappeared, along with their families, and within a few weeks my English friend Alison and her brother Paul, too. Mama could offer no explanation, other than that they had tried to get back home. I didn't think so, because Alison and Paul's house had been left with furniture still in it and their dog Sam had been abandoned in the garden. Alison and Paul would never leave Sam behind. We gave him a little bread and filled his bowl with water and promised him we would call by every day. Within a few weeks he had gone, too.

Most days I would call on my other friends from Holland, Belgium and England, but soon there was no one left. I was very sad and eventually I gave up. At least I still had my Javanese friends.

It was when I was walking home through the *kampong* one afternoon that I first saw the Japanese soldiers. From the very beginning I was terrified. They were all dressed in khaki uniforms and had jumped down from a lorry. They were running around and shouting at some men carrying bags and making them get into the lorry. The men looked terrified as the Japanese soldiers poked them with the huge knifes attached to their rifles. I hid behind a rubber tree and shook with fear, unable to move. I hardly dared breathe. When the frightened men were on board, the Japanese soldiers jumped up again and the lorry drove off.

The noises from the back of the lorry carried to my ears on the wind until it had disappeared from view. That was my first experience of the Japanese and the one thing I recall above all else was that the Japanese soldiers did not talk; they simply shouted or yelled. There was no talking at all. After the lorry disappeared, a cloud of dust seemed to hang in the air forever. I stayed behind the rubber tree until the dust had settled and I could see that the lorry and those nasty khaki men had gone, then I ran all the way home to tell Mama what I had seen.

One night, on 7 October 1942, Mama was rushed to hospital and gave birth to a beautiful boy, my brother Lars Hilmar. We called him Lasse. Papa insisted on coming home to look after his girls, but was not allowed to see his son in hospital. Both Karin and I were very upset and wondered why. Mama just said, 'It is his own fault.' Of course he came anyway, but they weren't happy together, which was sad. They should have been over the moon having produced such a beautiful, healthy baby.

Our extended family moved again to a nice house in 'Scandinavia Street'. It was cosy yet airy and light, with five rooms and a nice garden. Karin and I shared a fair-sized bedroom and we all seemed to enjoy a sort of normality. Except for the Japanese soldiers; they were everywhere, like swarms of little khaki ants. They never smiled, and yelled everywhere they went.

CHAPTER 2

Japs in Our Garden

❧

We were sitting on the terrace. It was a warm morning, but still quite fresh, and the sun was just beginning to rise over the hills, casting an orange glow over the garden. I sat with Papa and Karin drinking ice-cold orange juice. Mama had taken Lasse to the toilet indoors. It was a morning just like any other when we were disturbed by the familiar rumbling of a lorry trundling up the lane. On the front of the lorry, attached just above the headlight, was the setting sun of the Japanese flag.

The mere sight of it sent a shiver up my spine. The lorry drove to our neighbour's garden gate and stopped. I was aware that Papa was frozen with fear; he pulled Karin and me towards him tightly and wrapped a strong arm around each of us. Two Japanese soldiers jumped from the back of the lorry and ran into the garden of Mr Hansen. Mr Hansen was a Danish man who worked at the factory with Papa. He was sitting on his terrace with his wife Ingrid and his little boy Jon. Jon sat on his daddy's

7

knee and, as the Japanese soldiers ran up the garden path, Mr Hansen remained seated. One of the soldiers lunged at little Jon, pulled him by the arm and threw him forcibly onto the wooden floor of the terrace. The little boy bounced like a ball and landed in a heap with his little bottom up in the air and his face in the dust. Mrs Hansen screamed and Mr Hansen stood up to say something to the soldiers in protest, but before he could open his mouth one of the soldiers hit him in the face with his rifle.

Mr Hansen fell to the bottom of the steps, dazed and bleeding. Mrs Hansen screamed at the soldiers to stop as she went to the aid of her frightened and shocked son. The Japanese soldiers were shouting at Mr Hansen, telling him to move and poking him with their bayonets, shouting at him that he had to get on the lorry and that he was a prisoner.

It was simply the most awful thing I had ever seen. There was blood on Mr Hansen's shirt, but he managed to raise himself to his feet and put his hands above his head as he stumbled towards the lorry. The Japanese soldiers ran alongside poking him and, as he got to the lorry, other men's hands reached down and helped him up. We sat for a few minutes in silence while the soldiers checked some papers.

Mama joined us on the terrace and, from Mama and Papa's discussion, I could tell that Mama had seen everything from the kitchen window. Papa stood up and casually announced that he would be next. He walked inside and Karin and I started crying, not knowing what to expect.

Papa had packed a small bag a few days earlier with what he

called 'essentials'. He had his toothbrush, a razor, soap, a change of clothes and as much food as he could fit in. The bag was full of small tins, bars of chocolate and dried fruit. Papa returned, put the bag on the deck of the terrace and waited. He kissed us all very quickly and said goodbye. He told me to take care of Karin and that we weren't to worry because the war would be over in a few months and we would all be together again. My eyes filled with tears but I tried to be strong and not cry. He picked up his bag and walked to meet the Japanese soldiers, who had rushed into our garden after kicking down the gate. The soldiers were still shouting but Papa had prepared well and held out his passport as they approached him. They took a quick look and pointed to the lorry. Papa was very dignified; he didn't run, he walked, threw his bag onto the floor of the truck and climbed in. As the lorry started moving, Karin and I threw ourselves into Mama's arms and the tears flowed.

As the lorry drove away, I couldn't resist one last look, though I wish I hadn't. I strained to catch one last glimpse of Papa, but he had disappeared. The lorry was full of frightened men, packed in like sardines in tins. They were all standing, some were crying and their eyes looked out as if pleading for help. But there was none.

Scandinavia Street was eerily quiet, quieter than I could remember; even the birds had stopped chirping their morning chorus.

Later that day Mama prepared a couple of bags. She also made two rucksacks for me and Karin and, before she started packing them, I noticed her cutting into the rucksacks, then sewing them up again. Mama told us that we needed to prepare like Papa and not make the Japanese soldiers angry as Mr Hansen had.

'Are we going with Papa?' I asked.

Mama looked at me and shrugged her shoulders. 'Perhaps,' she said. 'I really don't know.'

'Are we going to prison?' asked Karin.

Mama smiled and shook her head. 'No, little one,' she said. 'We aren't going to prison; we are going to a camp where we will be safe until after the war.'

I told Mama I wanted to stay at home because we were safe here. We had a shelter at the bottom of the garden that would protect us from the bombs and the Japanese soldiers.

Mama didn't answer any more questions, even though I asked and asked. In the end I gave up and helped her carry the bags onto the terrace.

The bags were there for two days before the lorries turned up again and ordered us out of our home. We were prepared; so, too, were Mrs Hansen and little Jon; and although the Japanese soldiers shouted at all of us as we walked down the garden path, they didn't hit us or stab us with their horrible bayonets, as they had with Mr Hansen.

Mama, Karin and Lasse were helped up onto the lorry and Mama stood up and told me to throw my rucksack up. It was awfully heavy, but with all of my strength I heaved and threw it in her direction. I watched in disappointment as it hit the leg of an older woman and bounced back out onto the ground, rolling down into the ditch that ran the length of the road.

'Go now!' a Japanese soldier shouted. 'Leave . . . go.'

Things seemed to stop, as if frozen in time. I looked up at Mama; her eyes were fixed in the direction of the rucksack lying in the ditch. Her eyes told me that the bag was more important to her than anything else in the world; they were crying out with disappointment and fear. She looked at the Japanese soldier.

'Leave it, Lise,' she whispered. 'Up here quickly.'

'Go now,' the Japanese soldier hissed at me.

I couldn't leave it; Mama had taken such care packing the bag and I was more than a little curious about why she'd cut and sewed it so carefully. Instinctively I knew the rucksack was very special, so I darted past the soldier and scrambled into the ditch to retrieve it. As I reached the bag, a scream from the back of the lorry caused me to look up. The Japanese soldier was standing over me, holding his rifle up in the air. He was ready to hit me, yelling at me in Japanese. As he swung his rifle through the air, I ducked and it glanced off the rucksack harmlessly. Before he had time to recover, I darted past him as fast as my small legs would carry me. In one quick movement I'd thrown the rucksack to Mama and dived through her legs, scuttling to the front of the lorry. I could hear the Japanese soldiers shouting – some of them were laughing – but before any of them could come after me the lorry had started its engine and begun to move.

Mama was very angry with me and yet I could tell by the way she clung tightly to the bags that I had done the right thing.

There was no room to sit down in the lorry. It was packed tightly, the same as the lorry Papa had been taken away in. It was hot and my legs ached as we drove for hour after hour. I asked Mama for water but she would only give me enough to wet my lips, telling me we had to conserve it. The lorries kept stopping to pick up more prisoners. Poor Lasse cried for the whole journey as little beads of perspiration poured down his face, but he seemed to get more water than anyone else. Some of the other women on the truck had no water and asked the driver to stop in the villages we drove through.

The driver did not stop, even when some of the women started to cry.

I was aware of some women and children collapsing, which made it even worse as people were pushed out of the way. It became hard to breathe, especially with all of the dust coming up through the sides of the lorry. But still the lorry drove on. Just when I thought I could take no more we stopped. I looked at Mama and she smiled.

'We are here,' she whispered.

I looked at my brother and sister. Karin and Lasse were filthy, like little coal miners, with white eyes and black faces. Being so small they had suffered most with the dust and dirt in the bottom of the lorry. Lasse's face was streaked with tears; they looked like two little white rivers on either side of his face.

We drove through the gates into what looked like a big village with a huge fence around it and barbed wire on top. Dozens of Japanese soldiers stood spaced out a few metres from the fence. They never smiled; they looked angry and every one of them had a bayonet fixed to the top of his rifle.

CHAPTER 3

The First Camp: De Wijk

~❧~

'*Tenko! Tenko!*' the guards shouted as we climbed down from the lorry. They hit some of the women with rifles. *Tenko! Tenko!* The children were crying and the soldiers pushed us in line until eventually, one by one, as if by magic, everyone bowed forward in the direction of a short, evil-looking Japanese man with a small moustache and glasses. Mama made us copy the other women and we all bowed, even Karin. Mama would tell me later that was what the Japanese called *tenko*, and the man in front of us was an officer.

We were made to stand in the full heat of the sun while they inspected our passports. It seemed to take forever. I honestly thought I was going to die, I was so thirsty and hungry, and every time I stole a glance at one of the little khaki men a shiver ran the length of my spine. The Japanese made us place our bags in front of the line but forbade us from touching them. I could see my bottle of water sticking out of one of the pockets, but each time I asked Mama if I could get it she said no, while watching the soldiers warily. I looked up at the sun and then at the bottle of water time and time again. It was torture.

'Why, Mama?' I asked. 'Just one drink.'

'No,' she said firmly.

Poor Mama. Lasse was now sleeping on her shoulder and Mama had draped one of her big floppy hats over his head to protect him from the sun. I held an arm around Karin's shoulders as she sobbed gently the whole time. The Japanese guards paced up and down the lines of women and children, and every so often they would take a family away towards the houses on the far side of the camp. The line seemed to get bigger and bigger, with lorries arriving every few minutes, and I thought our turn would never come. I asked Mama where the families were going and she said they were being given a house each. Mama had been right: we weren't going to prison; we were going to get a new house. Two Japanese guards came towards us and I thought at last it would be our turn, but it wasn't to be.

They took a girl out of the line. I had noticed her when we arrived. She had smiled and made a space for me next to her. She had a pretty smile and I thought how nice it would be to have a big sister like her. As the two guards walked her away, a lady Mama's age walked towards the soldiers and began to protest loudly. One of the Japanese soldiers turned round and rammed his rifle butt into her stomach. The poor lady collapsed in a heap, struggling for breath. She burst out crying and wailing, pleading with the soldiers, and Mama rushed to her aid, telling her to be quiet.

14

'My baby,' she cried again and again. The Japanese soldiers continued to walk away, each one taking the arm of the girl, who was now crying and pleading for her mama to help. She'd fallen to the floor and the soldiers were now dragging her. They pulled her all the way to a hut at the far side of the compound, kicked open the door and bundled her inside. The two Japanese soldiers walked in after her and slammed the door behind them.

The lady was nearly hysterical now and a few of the other women were trying to calm her down. We could hear screams from the hut and each one sent a shiver up my spine. The remaining Japanese soldiers stood grinning and laughing. The more the poor lady cried, the more the soldiers laughed. A little later the girl was brought back to the line. Her mother ran to meet her and was quickly ushered back into line by the Japanese soldiers, who were still laughing. The poor girl was as white as a sheet and tears streaked her face. One of her eyes was swollen and some of her clothes had been torn away. I stared into her eyes; they were the eyes of a lost soul. I wanted to ask her why she had been punished when one of the soldiers shouted, 'Grønn-Nielsen.' Mama raised her hand and the soldier told us to follow.

The house we walked towards looked basic but pretty, with little window boxes on each window full of colourful flowers. I told Karin how nice it would be to get out of the sun, and when we got into our new house we would get something to eat and drink and then we could explore. Karin's eyes lit up and she picked up her tired pace a little.

The Japanese soldier pointed at the house and shouted, 'You

sleep here.' He looked at his papers again. 'Grønn-Nielsen, sleep here.'

Mama nodded and walked towards the front door. The Japanese soldier shouted again.

'No, there.' He pointed to a big olive-green door next to the house.

'There. Garage. Grønn-Nielsen family in garage.'

Before Mama could say anything he poked her in the back with his bayonet.

'Quick, now.'

He walked ahead of us and hit the door hard with the sole of his boot. The door burst open.

'Quick, you go.'

Mama's face fell in dismay as she peered into the space that was to be our home for goodness knows how long. The smell that hit me as I walked through the door made me cover my mouth with my hand: it smelt of oil, gasoline and dirty, sweaty men. The floor of the garage was covered in piles of rubble, car parts and general rubbish. It was dark and gloomy and I could make out the shape of an old car in the corner, though it was covered with dirty sheets and blankets.

We walked in. At the far end of the garage the door was broken and a huge dirty tarpaulin covered the gap. I pulled it to one side and could see the back of the house the garage was attached to and a small garden where two women sat talking.

Mama told us we must make the most of it and said we wouldn't be here long. I looked at her in amazement.

'We can't sleep here, Mama, there are no beds.'

Karin's smile had disappeared and all of a sudden her thirst and hunger had deserted her; she collapsed sobbing in the doorway, refusing to set foot inside. Mama ignored her and walked in. Lasse was still fast asleep on her shoulder and Mama handed him to me. She walked over to the far side of the garage, scanning the floor as she went. She found some empty cardboard boxes and pulled them apart, laying them on the floor of the garage. Then she pulled one of the blankets from the old car and laid them on top of the cardboard. She opened Lasse's bag and pulled out his coat, which she placed on top of the blanket.

'That will keep him clean,' she announced as she took him from me and laid him on the makeshift bed.

Mama made us work hard for the rest of the day as we cleaned the garage and made four beds from the cardboard and blankets that covered the car. I don't know how I slept in that filthy garage that first night, especially after I pulled at one of the blankets on the back seat of the old rusting car to reveal eight or nine squirming, hairless, day-old baby rats. My scream brought mama rat running to protect her young, and Mama was forced to beat her to death with a big hammer that was lying on the bonnet of the car. One by one we lifted the baby rats with a piece of cardboard and threw them outside. Mama didn't have the heart to beat the babies to death, but we watched as one by one they stopped moving in the heat of the sun.

After we had finished working we sat on our new beds and Mama gave us tinned fruit and biscuits, washed down with bottles of warm water. I must confess I felt a little better and more than a little excited at our new adventure that was just beginning. When it got dark Mama lit a candle, and a little later Lasse and Karin fell asleep. I tried to fight sleep by talking to Mama and asking her questions about the war and the camp and the girl who had been punished and the Japanese soldiers. Some questions she answered, others she didn't, just staring into space, but she reminded me again and again to stay away from the horrible Japanese soldiers.

'Don't talk to them,' she said. 'Don't even look at them. Just stay as far away from them as possible.'

It wasn't a bad dream.

The next morning I awoke in that horrible rat-infested garage. I closed my eyes many times and tried to sleep again, convincing myself that if I slept and woke again, I'd find myself in my beautiful bedroom back in Surabaya with my soft mattress, downy pillow and crisp white cotton sheets. It wasn't to be.

Karin burst out crying when she woke up. The noise woke Lasse and he joined in. What a noise!

Mama gave us tinned mandarins for breakfast and the sweet juice made us all feel better. We ate them just outside the door of the garage and the sunshine helped us to forget what our new living quarters were like inside.

In the fenced-off village, life seemed so normal. Mama said we were in one of the suburbs on the other side of Surabaya, though she didn't know exactly where. Mama was right. The village had a shop where you could buy fresh bread and tinned vegetables and fruit, sweets, water and orange juice, and people seemed to be going about their normal everyday lives. The only peculiarity was that this village had a huge fence surrounding it in every direction, patrolled regularly by the Japanese ant men who never smiled and always shouted. I walked up to the fence and looked out beyond.

More normality.

The village was on a slight incline and I looked down onto many railway lines with open-truck goods trains carrying crates of produce. The railway yard was separated by a busy dual carriageway, with lots of cars and bicycles. The railway lines stretched right to the sea, where the crates would be loaded onto ships. I could see the Javanese locals loading the trains and going about their normal business. Some laughed and joked, some sat in the shade taking a break, munching on bananas and mangoes with water bottles by their side. I couldn't help feeling that everything looked so familiar. I had been here before. Then it came to me. I looked at the dark grey building over the dual carriageway only three hundred metres away. It was a hospital; yes, I had been there before. I'd been there for an operation the previous year to have my tonsils removed. The beds had had soft mattresses and clean sheets and everything was nice. Mama had told me that the operation would make me a good girl and when I woke up from the operation, I asked if I was good. The nurses told me to whisper quietly as my throat would be sore. I explained to the nurse that Mama said I was a bad girl and the operation would make me better. The nurses did not look happy, and when Mama visited later that day there were words exchanged and she looked upset.

The last time I had seen that building I was free.

I took hold of the fence and pressed my face into the wire, asking myself what I had done to be made a prisoner? The wire bit into my skin and I winced in pain before drawing back. What had Mama and Papa done? We were nice people and we had never hurt anyone. We had a nice house and Papa worked hard. I thought about the garage and the rats and the smell of oil and the insects that crawled over my face in the middle of the night. I sank to my knees and my tears fell onto the parched earth. I felt hurt, degraded and helpless. The tears came to my eyes yet again, but I fought them back and replaced the feeling of self-pity with an overwhelming sense of anger and hatred towards our oppressors.

CHAPTER 4

Murder at De Wijk

I searched for Papa the whole of the first week but eventually gave up. There were quite a few men in the village at first, but eventually they disappeared one by one. Mama said the village was a camp that held prisoners temporarily until they were sent to labour camps further afield. She explained that the men were always kept separate from the women and children, and every few days they were rounded up and taken away on trucks. I witnessed emotional goodbyes as sons as young as twelve and thirteen were forcibly taken from their families by the Japanese. Whenever a mother or sister tried to intervene she would be beaten to the ground by the Japanese.

Every few days the inhabitants of each house were made to line up to take *tenko*. *Tenko* was silly and a waste of time and sometimes very cruel. The Japanese officers would stand everyone on parade in two or three lines and we were made to bow. We were shown exactly how far to bow: generally our heads would need to be as low as our hips. Mama said this was a mark of respect towards the Japanese officers. If anyone didn't bow correctly, they were hit in the middle of the back with a rifle butt without warning. The officers would parade in their finery and we wouldn't dare look any higher than the tops of the shiny leather boots that came up to their knees. Sometimes the *tenko* would last fifteen minutes, sometimes it would last far longer, and in the end people would collapse with exhaustion. I could never understand why they took so long when the paperwork and passports could be seen and checked in just a few minutes. Mama said that if ever I was out playing in the village and I came near to a Japanese officer I would need to step aside and keep on bowing until he walked away.

We had been there about a week when I woke with a start in the middle of the night. I heard voices coming from outside. I looked over towards the tarpaulin and, through a tiny two-inch gap, I could see outside to the garden. There were several women out there and they were on their hands and knees doing something in the ground. I strained hard to see who they were and what they were doing. The light of the quarter moon barely gave enough light to help them with whatever it was they were doing, but they continued slowly and carefully, speaking only in whispers. I stiffened in shock as I noticed a familiar shape. Then she spoke gently to one of the other women. She told her to hurry. It was the unmistakable voice of Mama.

I watched for another few minutes before I realized they were digging a hole. I was now kneeling at the gap in the doorway and had a good view of what they were doing. They were using their bare hands and one of the Dutch ladies was standing with several small cardboard boxes, which she held close to her chest. Mama said something to her and she crouched down. She handed three boxes to Mama and the other two ladies, and they exchanged pieces of paper. Then they placed the boxes into the hole and filled it with the dirt. When it was level they stamped it down with their feet and scattered some more dirt on top and a few loose stones. Afterwards they all shook hands. Then it came to me: they were burying treasure and the pieces of paper they exchanged were maps.

As Mama came back over towards the door, I quickly scuttled back into bed and pretended to be asleep. The next day I asked her what they had been doing and she explained that they had been hiding their valuables so that none of the Japanese could steal them. She warned me not to tell anyone.

One day we were out walking around the perimeter of the fence with Mama when three Japanese officers walked towards us. Mama ordered us to stop walking and we bowed. The Japanese officers walked past us and Mama stood up straight again. Suddenly we became aware of a commotion behind us. A tall man with bright red hair had walked past the officers and forgotten to bow. One of the Japanese officers yelled at him and the man yelled back. One of the Japanese officers drew his pistol and ordered the man to kneel at the officers' feet as he shouted and abused him. The man was trembling with fear. Mama picked up Lasse and ordered us away. She literally ran us back to the garage and bundled us inside. Mama breathed a sigh of relief as she pulled firmly at the garage doors to try and cut off the viewing platform and most of the unbearable noise and drama unfolding outside.

There were about forty people in the house attached to the garage where we lived and only one toilet. The toilet was right at the back of the house and there was always a queue stretching down the hallway. Some of the time the toilet had water, which took the waste away, other times it was dry. I had never smelled such a stench as I did each time I had to go. As the previous person left and I walked through the door, I held my nose and peered down into the bowl, praying it would be filled with water. Flies hung on the makeshift curtains and lamp shade and buzzed around my head as I sat down. It was simply the most disgusting room in the world and I dreaded the feeling that nature gave me every few days. Mama would always take care to wash our hands very carefully each time we came back from the toilet.

The days were very boring and long and revolved around one thing: food. Every day was a battle for survival. The Japanese provided two soup kitchens for the entire village. Twice a day a truck would come in with cabbages and rice, and occasionally some other green vegetables, too. Sometimes in the mornings we would get a little tasteless porridge with a crust of bread. The prisoners would be left to get on with preparation and cooking, and a rota was organized every few days. There was never any shortage of volunteers as the cooks would get the first few spoonfuls from the pot. Each soup kitchen had at least three big cooking pots made from cast iron. They were the size of a rain barrel and stained black from the smoke of the fires. The cooks would collect wood from around the compound and build fires under the pot that would burn for an hour. They were half-filled with water, which was brought to the boil, then the cabbages and rice would be thrown in. Occasionally a rabbit or a snake that had been caught would find its way into the pot, but the cooks would always take out the meat before we got to taste it.

Mama said that there was only enough soup for about a quarter of the people in the camp, and queues started forming as soon as the provisions arrived. Mama would send us out most days to queue for soup and rice while she looked after Lasse. Most of the time the soup ran out before our turn in the queue. When we were really hungry we would make sure we were one of the first in line. We'd get a bowl each and eat it on the way back, always saving just enough for Mama. Lasse seemed to have enough of his special powdered milk. Once Karin and I stood for nearly two hours and the soup ran out when there were only six people ahead of us in the queue.

It was survival of the fittest or, as Mama sometimes said, the luckiest. Some of the elderly women did not have the energy to stand in the heat of the sun for long periods and never queued at all. They grew weaker by the day unless their friends shared a little with them. Some of them just wasted away.

CHAPTER 5

Survival of the Fittest

We were fortunate we didn't starve in the first camp. I never felt really hungry for more than a couple of days, though what we ate was very basic. As if by magic Mama always seemed to find money from somewhere, and she would send Karin and me to the shop every day to stand in more long queues for fresh bread, fruit and occasionally smoked sausages. I would find out later that Mama had concealed money in our rucksacks, which we knew nothing about. At night she would unpick a little of the stitching and take out enough money for the next few days ahead, concealing it in her bra.

We were also very lucky to receive a food parcel from Uncle Axel every nine or ten days. It was like a Christmas present, with chocolate and tins of fruit, packets of rice and dried lentils. One week Aunt Marianne even put in a little doll each for Karin and me. Mama guarded those parcels with her life and there were always nasty glares and comments from the other women in the house, who were not lucky enough to receive parcels from friends outside. Mama would use the box as a pillow at nights until she could conceal the food in our other bags.

We also traded things for medicine with the local Javanese villagers on the other side of the fence, though this was not allowed by the Japanese, who would beat anybody they caught. Anything and everything was traded. We would give the Javanese blankets and clothes and in return they would supply us with fresh fruit and vegetables. Some of the women had no money and would sneak out in the hours of darkness to meet with the Javanese men and trade. The fence around the village was not very well secured in some places and at nights the soldiers would spend most of their time inside their huts drinking rice wine and playing cards. They were nearly always drunk. The women would lift the bottom of the fence and crawl underneath. Every so often the Japanese would catch them returning and punish them. Sometimes they dragged them away to their huts and other times they beat them there and then. Occasionally I heard a shot in the middle of the night, though Mama would never tell me exactly what had happened.

The Japanese had special holes dug into the sides of the embankments near the fence inside the camps. There was just enough room for one person and they had specially constructed wooden gates held in place by stakes hammered into the soil. The women who had been caught were thrown in these holes for several days without food and water. The other women risked their own lives to give them food and water when the Japanese were not around. If they were caught, they ended up in the holes as well. I remember Mama sneaking out of our garage late one night and, when I asked her where she had been, she explained that one of the girls in the hole was very ill. Mama told me she took her some water and a bar of chocolate, which the girl hardly had the energy to eat. She was released the next morning but died several days later. Mama cried for most of that day; the girl was only sixteen.

The village consisted of nine or ten streets, all fenced off from the outside world. The village became our playground and eventually Mama let me and Karin wander for most of the day while she sat guard at the entrance of our garage, protecting what little we had and looking after Lasse.

Many of the houses in the street still belonged to the families who'd originally owned them, but eventually the Japanese ordered them all to leave and sent them to other prison camps on the island. We learned to watch out for this, as the people were always ordered to vacate their houses in a hurry and were forced to leave most of their possessions behind. This was a signal for the children in the camp to move in and scavenge what they could. At first Karin and I resisted – I felt the other children were stealing – but after a few weeks, with pangs of hunger in my stomach and little by way of luxuries in our garage, I persuaded Karin to help me.

As the Japanese frogmarched a family away at the point of a bayonet, I waited until they were out of sight and then told Karin to run. We had to be quick as the houses were never empty for long. The door had been left unlocked and we ran quickly into the house, together with some adults and a few other children. It was a complete free-for-all, with people arguing with each other over the best of what had been left behind. While the others fought in the kitchen over tins of food and bottles of milk, I ran through to one of the back bedrooms and managed to get a fluffy white baby blanket, which I stuffed up my shirt. By the time I got back to the kitchen, the locusts had stripped the place bare. Karin was standing in the passageway, smiling and holding a box of biscuits and a cup and saucer.

Mama was absolutely horrified that her two darling girls had stooped to the level of a street thief. She quickly changed her mind, though, when we all lay on the soft blanket that evening munching on the delicious biscuits Karin had found. A few days later Mama traded the cup and saucer for six large bananas.

As the houses were cleared I became more and more cunning, watching the Japanese soldiers and looking for telltale signs that they were about to take a family away. The Japanese soldiers would always clear the houses in threes and I watched carefully for groups of three walking a little more quickly than they normally would. Sometimes they would be carrying sheets of paper with them, which I assumed had the name and address of the family to be removed, and generally they took families away early in the morning. I began to get up as soon as I woke up. When we first went to the camp there was nothing to get up for: no school, no nice breakfasts of ham and eggs and hot buttered toast like we used to get back in Surabaya. Breakfast in the camp was normally a dried biscuit or some fruit. Now I had a reason to get up.

Mama, Karin and Lasse would still be sleeping and I'd dress quickly and sit outside watching. The soldiers started to appear at first light and, not long after, would clear any houses that needed emptying. I'd follow along a good distance behind and pretend that I was walking in the direction of the shop. There were no other children around. The scene was very familiar. By this time most of the men had gone and the only people that came out of the houses were women and children. The women were always crying and a lot of the children too. Most had learned to be quiet, but still some protested. The Japanese guards would think nothing of hitting anybody who objected with the butt of a rifle.

Once the guards and the family were a safe distance away, I would run into the house and search it, taking everything I could carry. I took trousers for Lasse, socks and baby clothes, blankets and food. On other occasions I'd look for toys and pencils, crayons and paper to write on. I remember one day finding a skipping rope and, another day, a bicycle, which I rode proudly home to show Mama. I could tell that Mama wasn't overly keen on me bringing stuff home, but she accepted that if I didn't take the things then others would. I managed to find a mosquito net on one occasion and Mama's face lit up as she saw it. She constructed a little frame with wood and string and was able to protect Lasse during the hours of darkness.

Mosquitoes were always a problem and some nights they kept us awake for hours. I hated them. Just as I was falling asleep, they would buzz in my ears and no matter how hard I tried to get to sleep, it would be impossible. Other times they would wake me as they bit my arms and legs. I envied my little brother who had his own mosquito net now; I couldn't help feeling that perhaps it should have been me that got it. After all I had found it.

Mama would tell me to look for repellents and iodine in the houses that were being cleared and now and again I found some and enjoyed a peaceful night's sleep. Others were not so lucky and Mama told me that some of the children and their mamas had died from malaria and yellow fever. The Japanese never gave any medicine to the people who caught the diseases.

Mama had started asking me to look for specific things in the houses. One morning she asked me to find some shoes for Karin. Karin's shoes were too small for her and Mama had cut out the toes with a knife so they looked like sandals. Karin didn't like them; she said her shoes were broken.

Most of the children in the camp had no shoes as there was nowhere to buy any, and they would walk around the camp in bare feet. Any little cuts or insect bites would fester and the insects and flies would be attracted to the wounds. Some of the children's feet were in such terrible condition they couldn't even walk. About a week after Mama had asked me for some shoes, I awoke when it was still dark. I heard the voices of the little khaki ants and they were shouting. They were familiar words by now. Although I didn't know what they meant, they used them whenever they were taking people out of their houses. I heard a woman's voice crying and leapt to my feet. I dressed quickly and ran outside. One of the Japanese soldiers was kicking a little girl on the ground. She was no more than seven years old and her mama was crying and trying to stop him. Another soldier held her by the hair. I couldn't look and ran back into the house until the noise had died away. When I went back outside, it was very quiet and the sun was beginning to cast early morning shadows over parts of the camp. I wondered what street the family had been living in and walked in the general direction they'd come from.

As I turned the corner and looked at the houses in the street my eyes focused on one in particular. A slight breeze blew through the village and directly opposite where I stood a green door opened and closed gently in time with the wind. I paused and looked up and down the street. Every other door was closed . . . this had to be the house they had come from.

A pot of coffee stood on the kitchen bench, the steam floating gently up to the ceiling. I thought about taking it back for Mama – she loved coffee – but as I picked it up I realized it was too hot to carry. I searched through the bedrooms until eventually I found what I was looking for: a pair of black leather shoes that belonged to the little girl who had been attacked by the Japanese soldier. She was about the same age as Karin and roughly the same size. I held them up to the light at the window and prayed they'd fit.

I was so excited I took nothing else from the house. I just ran home as fast as my legs would carry me. Mama was still sleeping when I walked into the garage and I sat down beside her and stroked her hair. She woke up.

'What is it, dear?' she asked. 'Why are you looking so happy?' I held up the shoes and the two of us fell about laughing. Mama cuddled me and we woke Karin up with her early morning gift. They were a little too big, but Mama stuffed some paper in the toes and they fitted perfectly. Karin gave me a big kiss and a little later Lasse woke up, too. He had his mosquito net and Karin had her shoes. Next time it was Mama's turn for a present.

It was getting close to Christmas and I had an idea. A few days later I was up and about early again. I walked and walked around the streets, looking for a house for Mama's present. At last I spied a house with a door wide open. I watched for a few minutes and there was no movement to be seen. I approached the door cautiously, listening for any noise. It was quiet; the house was empty. I walked through the door and into the kitchen. There were biscuits on the table and beautiful china cups and plates, towels and tablecloths. I felt like Aladdin in his cave full of treasure and I couldn't wait to take my fill. My heart seemed to miss a beat as I heard the sound of a baby crying right behind me and I turned round in horror. The baby lay in a playpen in the next room and I froze as the sound of ladies' voices carried from a distant room. There were footsteps coming towards me now, louder and louder, and the baby's crying increased in tempo.

I ran into the passageway, looking for an escape, but stopped dead in my tracks as a big woman blocked my path and asked in Dutch what I was doing. I looked at the door to the street and wondered if I could beat her in a race. She looked angry and protective, and she wanted an answer. I feared she might take me to the Japs and accuse me of being a thief. She asked me again what I was doing.

I knew a Dutch woman who lived nearby called Nina.

'I'm looking for Nina,' I said. It was the first thing that came into my head.

The Dutch lady smiled. 'She's not here, young lady.' She pointed outside. 'Three houses down, you'll find Nina there.'

As I walked away, she shouted that I should knock the next time. I looked over my shoulder, smiled and said I would.

It was at least another two weeks before I plucked up the courage to explore an empty house again. It was a few days before Christmas and I simply had to get a present for Mama.

In the Scandinavian tradition we have our Christmas feast on Christmas Eve, when we are all together as a family. We have a special Norwegian dinner with all the trimmings, followed by coffee and cakes, while us children get busy opening numerous presents. Outside our house the previous year I could not help noticing how gloomy everyone was, but indoors, under the roof of our little house in Scandinavia Street, it was simply magical.

The Christmas tree that Papa had brought was beautifully decorated and sparkled. Our pretty house shone with flickering candles placed everywhere. We were quite proud of the special Christmas decorations we had made ourselves. The most impressive thing in all this was our beautiful small white piano. Karin and I had been practising for weeks and were anxiously waiting for the chance to play a couple of well-known Christmas carols.

Everyone agreed we played very well, and it was simply the best Christmas I could remember.

I was the only member of the family giving presents on Christmas Eve 1943 and I was very excited and proud of what I had managed to salvage from the empty houses. I wasn't concerned that I wouldn't be getting a present. I think Mama was a little sad, but she hid it well. She cut a thick branch from one of the trees outside and we decorated it with ribbons and pieces of paper that we'd coloured with crayons. Mama had kept back some apples, bananas and biscuits, but made a point of telling us that there would be no shows of extravagance this Christmas. Mama explained that we would be going to another camp soon and everything we had, including money, had to be carefully managed.

We talked about Papa late in the afternoon and Mama said that perhaps we would all be together next Christmas. I asked where Papa was and Mama said she didn't know but that she felt sure he would be safe because he could speak Dutch, German, French, English and Javanese, and a man who could speak so many languages was very valuable to the Japanese. She supposed he would be working in an office somewhere safe, and that he would have good food and a nice bed to sleep in every night.

Mama made us all feel better. As darkness drew in, she asked me to light the candles I'd taken from one of the empty houses. It sounds strange, but as it got dark we could have been spending Christmas Eve anywhere. We were warm and dry and had a feast of sorts, with cold sausages, bread and as much fruit as we could eat and, of course, the biscuits. We quietly sang a few carols and just before we went to bed I handed my brother and sister their presents. Lasse got a new jacket and a furry teddy bear. He turned his little nose up at the jacket, but his eyes lit up as he peeled the newspaper from his teddy bear. He pulled it up to his face and stroked the soft fur. Within a few minutes he was fast asleep. Karin was overjoyed with her dolly and a bar of milk chocolate, but the biggest smile of the evening belonged to Mama. I had wrapped several sheets of newspaper carefully around her gift and she laughed as she peeled each layer away. Slowly but surely her almost-new silk scarf, finely stitched with colourful butterflies, came into view. She put it to her face and breathed in deeply before draping it around her neck. She told me it was the best present she had ever had, and even in the flickering light of the strategically placed candles I could see that her eyes were filled with tears.

CHAPTER 6

Monsoons, Malnutrition and Disease

❧❧❧

The joy of Christmas was quickly forgotten when the monsoon rains arrived soon after. The first memory I have is of my home-made wooden crate bed floating in several centimetres of water when I woke up. The rains had arrived in the middle of the night and within a few hours had seeped under the door of the garage, bringing a host of creepy-crawlies, mud and human waste from a broken sewerage pipe.

The smell hit me first – it was like nothing I'd smelled before – and as poor Karin awoke a few seconds after me she cried out in fright, upended her little bed, and fell into the stinking mess. Her screams woke Mama and Lasse and before long we were desperately salvaging what we could, lifting everything onto the bonnet of the old car and the oil drums in the corner. All the blankets and my special pillow were soaked and stained with the brown sludge that seemed to be getting deeper by the minute. Mama collected everything together and ran out in the rain to hang everything up. Afterwards, she looked out of the back door and watched the rain pounding into the ground.

'At least it will get a good wash.' She smiled.

Within an hour the whole village looked like a giant swimming pool and still the rain continued. It rained non-stop for two days. There were no supplies brought in and no soup kitchen and for two whole days we stayed in the garage, ate what fruit was left and the remaining biscuits and chocolate from Uncle Axel's parcels. We slept in the dirty old car. At least it was dry, but I couldn't help thinking about the baby rats wriggling and squeaking centimetres from the very spot where I laid my head. When the rain stopped, the sun appeared and within an hour the pillow and blankets were bone-dry. Mama announced that the rainy season had arrived and we must construct our beds as high off the floor as possible. We managed to build a platform from broken wooden crates and cardboard, which we placed on four oil drums, and Mama lifted us onto it each evening before climbing up herself. It took many weeks before the stench in the garage disappeared and the ground dried out completely.

It was during the rainy season that I first noticed Mama's health deteriorate. She awoke each morning, stiff as the crate she was lying on, complaining about pains in her back and shoulders. Sometimes the pain would spread to her hands and elbows, too. Mama found it very difficult to carry Lasse any great distance and her occasional walks around the village compound stopped altogether. She would shoo us out of the garage and make us take Lasse out while she lay on the crate and stared at the ceiling. It was not nice to see; it was as if Mama had given up.

It was six o'clock in the morning and pitch-black when I heard the Japs outside.

'*Cepat, cepat* [quickly],' they shouted in Indonesian, but this time it was different. As we stumbled outside into the darkness, half asleep, they told us to get our belongings. Mama smiled.

'At last,' she said, 'we're leaving this place.' We quickly gathered up everything we could carry and made our way over to the compound gate.

'*Tenko, tenko*,' they shouted and we obeyed. We were still doing *tenko* as the sun came up and we stood in exactly the same position as the sun developed its early morning heat. I looked at poor Mama as the sweat trickled from her chin and fell onto the dust. She was clearly in agony with her aches and pains. Mama kept looking at me, trying to muster a smile.

'Don't worry,' she said. 'It's true, the ladies are telling me we are leaving here today.' It was the only thing that kept us going.

At last the Japanese officer gave the order to stand. My back seemed to be locked into that awful position and it took an eternity before I was able to right myself. Mama gasped in pain as she too regained her standing position. By early afternoon people were sitting around on their bags, but some had fainted through lack of water and the intense heat. The Japs made no attempt to move them and still refused us food and water. Lasse had been crying and sobbing constantly for over an hour as he sat in between us. Mama and I took turns to hold his hand and give him little sips of water – thank goodness we had brought a few bottles. He sat with Mama's huge oversized hat to shade him from the sun, playing with the little stones in the dirt.

The Japs made us sit by the fence as a lorry pulled up and the gates opened. At last, I thought, we were going. No one told us where we were going, though there were plenty of rumours. Some ladies said we were going to be freed and some said we were going to another camp many hours away. Some even whispered that our time was up, whatever that meant. The black asphalt we sat on was burning hot and after a few minutes it was worse than doing *tenko*. I wondered whether the Japs had made us sit there deliberately. As I shuffled towards the dirt surface one of them ordered me to be still. It was agony and I could see Mama and Karin were suffering, too. Lasse sat on my knee and, as the Japs looked away, we shuffled inch by inch towards the relative coolness and comfort of the dirt.

Sadly we were going nowhere. Not that day anyway. A Jap officer came out of the hut by the gate shouting in broken English.

'Not today,' he yelled. 'Not today. Back to house.'

As I walked away my arms, legs, back and shoulders screamed out in agony.

When we arrived back at our garage there were three women in there and they refused to leave. I had never seen them before. We were told they had entered almost as soon as we were ordered out that morning and that they had spent the day making themselves at home. They had come from an overcrowded house two streets away. They were Dutch, middle-aged, and two of them were slightly overweight. One of them looked very determined as she announced that our garage was now their garage and that she was going nowhere. Mama tried to reason with them, but it was no good. She asked where her children would sleep, but the determined lady just said, 'That's your problem, not mine.' Mama pointed out to the ladies that some of our belongings were still there, as if to prove to them that it really was our house.

Just as we had given up hope, another woman arrived. It was the leader of the house next door. She stormed into the garage and ordered the women to leave, confirming that the garage was ours and that children always took priority. At first the three ladies protested, but she stood her ground and was very forceful. Eventually they collected their baggage and left. As the determined one turned round and glared at me, I couldn't resist giving her a little wave and a smile, behind Mama's back, of course. Mama thanked the lady who had helped us and we settled down in our home once again.

A few mornings later we repeated the whole exercise. It was early morning and the Japs told us we were leaving. They gave us ten minutes to collect our belongings and get to the gate for *tenko*. Mama did not look well and appeared very stiff with her pains, rubbing at the back of her neck and the joints of her elbows. I made Karin collect the tins of food and pack her rucksack. Mama slowly got Lasse's bag packed while I packed my rucksack and made a big bundle of all the things I thought would be useful: the mosquito net, some plates, a pillow and three bottles of water. I wrapped them all up in a big blanket and tied it up with string. I left a gap at the top and managed to squeeze a stick through, then lifted it up onto my shoulder. It was heavier than I thought and I wished for a second that I hadn't packed so much water.

I lifted my rucksack onto the other shoulder and stood up straight.

'C'mon, Mama, we must go.'

Mama smiled, picked up Lasse and we walked outside.

We sat down at the large gate. There were a lot of people and Mama was sobbing gently, massaging her back with her fingers every few minutes. Lasse cried and Karin complained about being hot, thirsty and tired. After three hours we were sent back to our garage.

A week later we went through the same thing, and once again we were sent back to our squalid little garage, tired and dejected. As I looked around I prayed to myself that we would get away from there soon.

Another seven days passed and the Japs turned up at six in the morning and instructed us to line up at the gate for *tenko* with our belongings. As we approached the gate I noticed that five lorries were parked in a line on the road outside.

CHAPTER 7

Escape from De Wijk

After six months living in a dirty garage at De Wijk holding camp, at last we were on our way.

The atmosphere in the back of the lorries was one of cautious optimism. Most of the ladies had heard that we were to be moved to family camps that had been specially constructed. No more dirty garages and sleeping on boxes, no more rats or floods in the night. The kitchens at the camps were better organized, too, one lady said, with more food and better hygiene. We were in the back of the lorry for no more than two hours. Although it was cramped and there wasn't room for everybody to sit down, I managed to gently push a space around us, allowing Mama to sit on our rucksacks. I handed her Lasse and he fell asleep in her arms. I think Mama managed to doze a little, too; she had looked so weary lately and had been complaining that the pains had been waking her up at nights. She blamed the dampness in the garage. As I watched her sleeping, I smiled. We were going to a new camp, somewhere cleaner and drier where Mama would get better again. When she woke she drank lots of water. I gave water to Karin and Lasse, too, but thought it better not to take any for myself as all the bottles were only half full now. I was hot and thirsty but I could wait a little longer.

The lorry had stopped and, as always, the Japs were shouting and barking out their commands. Why must they be so loud and aggressive? I thought to myself. As we climbed from the lorry I could see we were at a railway station.

The familiar cry went up again. *Tenko! Tenko!*

There were hundreds of women and children lined up, bowing, outside the station and many Japs with pieces of paper shouting out the names of the different families. It seemed like chaos. We stood around for about an hour before our names were called and then we were marched inside the station. We were made to stand in line in groups of about fifty. Some of the ladies were asking the Japs for food and water and some were asking for the toilet. One lady was trying to explain to a soldier that she had been on the lorry for hours and her little boy was severely dehydrated. As he lay in her arms he didn't even have the strength to cry. The Jap soldier slapped her across the face, made her get back in line and walked away.

There were trains coming into the station every fifteen minutes and groups of people were then ordered onto the coaches. The ladies complained that there wasn't enough room, but the Japs just shouted at them and hit some of the ladies with their rifle butts, kicking and punching anyone who protested. It was all too much for me. I turned my head away and buried it in Mama's chest.

When it was our turn, we were pushed up to the top of the station. Karin was asking to go to the toilet but Mama couldn't see one. I noticed some of the smaller children using the station walls as a toilet and that made me realize I needed to go, too. When we got to the top of the platform there were two queues forming. I quickly realized that one was for the lone toilet on the platform and the other was for a tap where people were filling water bottles. I took two of our water bottles and joined a queue of about forty people, while Mama joined the queue for the toilet.

We stood in the queues for no more than two minutes before the train rumbled into the station and, with a screech of brakes, came to a stop right next to us. It was a signal for the Japs to move us.

'On train,' they shouted. 'Move. Train now.'

I was in a panic; how long were we going to be on the train? We needed more water. The Japs were pushing people away from the tap and one woman who protested was hit on the side of the head with a rifle. Her head split open and blood poured from the wound. Everyone in the queue had turned around as she screamed and I took the opportunity to run to the front. I managed to fill one and a half bottles before a fat woman noticed me and pulled me away by the collar. She barely had time to get her own bottle under the tap before she was pushed away by a soldier. She glared at me as we were herded towards the train.

I panicked as I couldn't see Mama or my brother and sister, but then I spotted them at the entrance to the truck and ran towards them. I held up the two bottles of water to show Mama I had been successful. She tried to give me a smile, but it wouldn't come.

Poor Mama. She explained that no one had been to the toilet. Some of the ladies were squatting down on the platform in desperation. The Japs looked on with great amusement, smiling and pointing at the women as the platform became awash with hot, steaming urine. More and more ladies took the opportunity to relieve themselves. I could not describe the look on the faces of the Japs. I had not seen the look before; they were fascinated and, although they were still forcing people onto the train, they seemed to be taking their time so that more and more women would be forced into the ultimate humiliation.

You can't imagine that train journey, which would last for nearly twelve hours. The Japanese soldiers beat the people into the train. As we cried out for mercy and begged them not to put any more families into the truck, they loaded more. The crush was unimaginable as the last few people shied away from the Jap rifle butts, swinging and flailing around in the doorway. As the soldiers bolted the door from the outside the panic subsided a little and we were able to breathe more easily. But before the train departed we stood at the station for at least an hour.

The heat was unbearable as the full sun beat down on the train roof. There were four small windows high up on each side of the train, but the air was still and humid. I started to sweat after just a few minutes, the beads of perspiration dropping from my chin in regular four-second intervals. I counted again and again until they started falling every three seconds. There was no room to sit down, but I squashed and pushed a little in order to put our rucksacks on the floor. I told Karin she would have to stand and gave her the half-bottle of water, which seemed to comfort her. She took a long gulp and I told her to be careful as it was all we had. I then managed to ease Mama on top of the rucksacks so that she could take the pressure off her legs. Lasse lay on her lap.

I heard a thud on the carriage floor, then another, and someone called out for a nurse. Two of the older ladies had fainted. The crush started again as people moved and made way for a lady who had declared herself a nurse. I watched through the tangled web of legs as the nurse worked on one lady, then the other, managing to breathe life back into them. The train lurched and with a loud clunk jerked forward and began to move. Much later, I recall, as the train came to a stop, a wave of urine flowed down the truck floor, soaking our shoes. As the train started to move again the pool came back the other way. Our rucksacks were now soaking wet and the foul smell of ammonia filled the air. Thankfully, as the train picked up speed, air flowed through the open windows and very slowly the temperature decreased until it became more bearable.

I tried to think of reasons why people would place us in such conditions when we had done nothing wrong. I thought that surely the train would stop and someone would announce that there had been a terrible mistake, but the horror went on. After several hours I located a tiny space on a wooden bench by the side of the carriage. I squeezed in between two ladies and pushed little by little until I felt there was enough room for Mama, then I told her to quickly take my place. I pulled her down between the two ladies. They weren't happy, but she smiled at each of them as I handed Lasse to her and he flopped onto her lap. It was a tight fit, but Mama looked so much more comfortable than on her seat on the rucksacks.

By now the carriage had become stale with the smell of sweat and the bladder contents of people who could hold it in no longer. Then the temperature started to increase again. As the train picked up speed and nature took its course, the women and children had no option but to let loose the contents of their bowels where they stood. The stench was worse than anything I had ever smelled, and soon the floor was awash with a foul brown sludge. The smell made some of the children vomit, adding to the problem. Then the flies descended on us.

I don't know where they came from; they just seemed to swarm through the windows, the smell bringing them in from miles around. At first I knocked them from my face, swatted at them with my water bottle, but in the end I was so exhausted I gave up and let them crawl all over me. Mama had covered Lasse with the mosquito net, and although the flies hovered and crawled over it, he slept peacefully in his own little cocoon. Oh, how I wished I could be Lasse, oblivious to everything that was going on around him. How I wished I could be in my dear little garage with a nice bed, space, food and water and a toilet I could use. Suddenly the horrible garage didn't seem so horrible after all. I slept a little as the temperature began to rise again and I dreamed of our house in the suburb of Surabaya with the green garage door and the beds made of wood and cardboard and my pillow and cool water from the tap outside.

I awoke with a start. Karin was pulling at my sleeve.

'I need more water,' she said.

I scolded her and told her that she had had a bottle to herself and there was no way I could give her any more. She started crying and confessed that her bottle had simply disappeared before the train even started moving. Mama had been listening to the conversation and was angry with Karin.

'How many times have I told you to guard the bottles with your life?' she said in a raised voice. 'You silly little girl.'

Karin apologized and said she'd fallen asleep holding the bottle to her chest as she leaned into Mama. Someone had taken advantage of the opportunity and stolen it from her. I gave her the last few mouthfuls from my bottle, gave a little to Lasse and wet my lips with what was left. We were now completely out of water and still the train trundled on. As well as being desperate for more water, I had cramp in my stomach. I didn't know how long we had been moving, but nature was telling me I had to eat. I went into my rucksack and took out the last banana, which I peeled and divided into four. It tasted so good as we nibbled tiny bits and tried to chew them for as long as we could, but eventually they disappeared.

'Surely it can't be long now, Mama,' I said.

She stroked Lasse's hair but didn't bother to answer. Lasse sucked his two middle fingers and for once looked at ease. It's amazing how good a little water and a quarter of a banana can make you feel.

At last the train came to a stop. We were at a station called Semarang. As the Japs opened the door to the carriage, we almost fell out onto the platform. It felt as if I had stood in the same position for the whole journey, even though I had swapped places with Karin. My legs had forgotten what it was they were supposed to do and the other ladies and children were the same. Some fell over onto the station; others held each other up, unable to put one foot in front of the other. Karin was frozen to the spot, complaining about pins and needles in her legs, and Mama looked just awful.

There were Japs everywhere, more than I had ever seen before, and they were aiming their guns at us. Some were shouting and some were laughing at the women sprawled on the ground. I spotted it before anyone else. I grabbed our two remaining water bottles and made a bolt for the tap. I'd filled one bottle before anyone noticed and was well on the way to filling up the second before someone's hands were on me, trying to pull me away. They simply refused to allow me to get the bottle anywhere near the tap. I replaced the rubber stoppers and took the water over to Mama. We shared one bottle between us there and then, and Mama put the remaining one in her holdall.

The women and children were all on their feet now, breathing in the fresh air and trying as best they could to clean themselves with dried sand. The stink still lingered in the air, but at least it kept the Japs at a safe distance. I think that even they were shocked at what we looked like. The flies buzzed above our heads and no one had escaped the brown sludge. It was all over our feet and legs, but the women who had fainted had fared much worse. Women were begging the Japs for food for their children, but they just pointed to the water tap. Those with bottles filled them up and those without drank from the tap until they could drink no more. I joined the queue again and managed to fill another bottle before the Japs ordered us away with their bayonets.

Outside the station we were made to *tenko* again. What was it with these men, I thought, that they needed to have respect shown to them so often? Mama said they had such low self-esteem that they needed to display the power they had over us time and time again. It made them feel good, powerful. I didn't think it was such a great show of power that they could control women and small children, and that they needed guns and bayonets to do so. I comforted myself with the thought that such a pathetic band of men would surely not win the war.

CHAPTER 8

A Long Way to the Church.
The Second Camp: Bangkong

~~❧~~

February 1944

We set off on the long march in the blazing early afternoon sunshine, in groups of twenty-five with five guards assigned to each. We had not been given any food and were told there were no lorries to take us to our final destination. We walked and walked and walked, sipping gently at our water bottles until they were empty. We passed through villages as the locals just stood and stared. We begged them for food and water, but they gave us none; Mama said they would be shot if they made contact with us. To me they looked almost as hungry and tired as we were, and I could see their bones through their skin.

Women and children were starting to collapse, but the guards just kicked at them on the floor until they raised themselves up or others from the group lifted them up and supported them.

The thing I remember most about that march was the total

lack of noise; no one had the energy even to talk. Children were no longer crying, there was just an occasional groan or whimper, as if to say, I'm still alive, I'm still here, don't forget me. No one talked except to ask permission to go to the toilet. When that happened a soldier would disappear with the poor woman who needed to go. It happened with Mama. She told me the horrible little man watched her relieve herself, grinning all the while through his thick spectacles. Thank goodness I didn't have to go.

I could see Mama was on the verge of collapse. She was swaying gently and rocking from side to side, and every so often she would stamp down hard on the ground, as if she had fallen asleep while walking. It was as if her body was reminding her that it wasn't a good place to rest: stay on your feet, it cried to her. I bit my bottom lip and held back the tears that wanted to fall. Why did I have to watch Mama like this? Why did I have to carry Lasse? He was so, so heavy. And why did Karin have to whimper so much? But still Mama battled on, placing one foot in front of the other again and again. She stared straight ahead as the flies crawled around her lips and entered her open mouth. I so wanted to give her water, but I had none; I wanted to support her but didn't have the strength. Thankfully some of the stronger ladies helped her.

We walked through more villages and the reaction of the inhabitants was always the same. They watched from a safe distance. The women were pleading for food and water, but the villagers showed no emotion and didn't move a muscle. I concentrated on looking at the dusty road and willing my feet to move. One step at a time, I told myself. The shadows dancing around at my feet were longer now; darkness would be with us soon.

We walked on and on in silence. I tried to concentrate on the road but my eyes were drawn towards Mama. She was clearly in a serious condition and at times even walked with her eyes closed. I held her by her arm and tried to guide her as best I could, but still she rolled from side to side. I had carried Lasse now for at least an hour, but I didn't dare give him to Mama to hold. I knew the weight of my brother would bring her to her knees and I couldn't bear to see the Japs kick at her exhausted body. Just when I thought Mama could not take another step, the guards began talking to each other and pointing up ahead. We were approaching another village and something told me that if we did not stop and get some food and water and rest a little, Mama would not make it out of there.

In the middle of the village was a church with steps leading up to a big wooden door. The soldiers ordered us to sit on the steps and two of them knocked on the door and disappeared inside. Karin collapsed on the steps in tears and I handed Lasse to her. I eased Mama on to the steps and joined her. Never did I think that a rough stone step would seem so comfortable; it was like sinking into the softest armchair in the world and I lay back and stretched onto the cool stone. I gazed up into the sky at the twinkling stars and wanted to be somewhere up there on a distant planet. I wanted to be anywhere but here.

The Japs came out after a few minutes and ordered us into the church. It took me a few minutes to get Mama up and, with all the energy she could summon, she walked the half-dozen steps into the doorway before lurching forward and collapsing in a heap. Karin and Lasse started crying and I confess I didn't know what to do. Before I had a chance to do anything, three or four women were around her and one tried to pour water into her mouth. Her eyes were closed and her head flopped like a rag doll. One of the Japs moved forward, pointing and shouting, and I thought he was about to kick her as he had the other ladies who had collapsed on the march. I moved myself between him and poor Mama and took a firm grip on my empty water bottle. I was so, so frightened. Part of me wanted to protect Mama and part of me wanted to take my water bottle, hold it above my head and tell the horrible little man that he would get it across his head if he came near her. I wanted to tell him that if he laid one finger on her he would have a headache for a week. The water bottle stayed frozen at my side. I was powerless and scared out of my mind, and I realized that a water bottle was little use against an evil Jap soldier and his bayonet. Before he got near us I was pulled out of the way as one of the ladies shouted to him, 'Hospital, hospital.'

They argued for a few seconds and eventually a stretcher was found and Mama was taken away. The Japs were still shouting out their protests as they left and the huge doors slammed shut, plunging the church into darkness.

A nice lady, who I later found out was a nun, welcomed us to the Church of the Virgin Mary. She told us Mama would be fine; she needed to wash, drink lots of water and eat a little food. She would be back with us in a few hours.

She looked at the three of us and said, 'And you must wash, too. Cleanliness is next to godliness.'

I had been thinking about God a lot on that march . . . I wondered when he would show up and help his little children.

The nun took us outside to the church garden and helped us strip down to our underwear. We washed and drank lots of water at the same time, then we put on clean clothing from our rucksacks and she helped to dress Lasse. Already we were beginning to feel better, and after we had washed and changed we lined up for cabbage soup and bread. Afterwards Lasse was given a banana. Karin and I so wanted a banana, too, but the lady explained that only boys and girls under two were allowed a banana each day. I wondered if Lasse might share his as he munched on it as if he had never seen a banana in his life. Karin and I watched him jealously as he smiled, cramming every last bit into his mouth. Poor Lasse, he didn't understand. I would have shared that banana with my brother and sister. Karin and I shared the skin. We split it in half and scraped it with our fingernails. It tasted so good and we scraped and scraped until eventually the sweet taste turned sour. We both knew we were down to the bare skin and that we had to throw it away or we would get stomach ache.

Mama appeared after a few hours and looked much better, although she was still very pale and weak. The ladies had fed her and she had been washed and changed. She was actually smiling and all three of us cuddled into her and wouldn't let go. We were then taken into the church and shown our sleeping quarters.

The church was very dark with no lights at all. There were a few candles on window ledges and one or two near the doorway. The lady who was showing us round pointed to the wooden benches where people had already started to bed down for the night. The benches were constructed of roughly sawn wood and sat about thirty centimetres from the ground. Each bench frame was about twenty metres long by two metres wide and there were four of them sitting in the church where I imagined the pews had once been. The benches in the middle were more or less full and I counted fifty-five women and children lying down together head to head, either sleeping or whispering gently to each other. The woman pointed to a space no more than two metres wide.

'You can sleep there,' she said and then wished us good night.

We walked over and lay our blankets down in our allocated space. Some of the other women did not look happy as we squeezed into the gap, causing them to shuffle along a few centimetres. I pushed our rucksacks under the bench and tied the straps underneath it; that way no one would be able to take anything through the night. I lay my head on the frame of the bench and, although it was a little uncomfortable, I fell asleep almost immediately.

It was the daylight coming in through the dirty windows that eventually woke me. As I lay still and looked up, I marvelled at the beautiful stained-glass windows depicting scenes from the Bible and wondered why they hadn't been washed for a long time. The rays of sun picked out the particles of dust in the air, gradually revealing the sorry state of over 200 weary souls.

CHAPTER 9

A Lullaby by Johannes Brahms

The Japs issued us with numbers made from cardboard, which we had to wear at all times. We were each given a large, rusty safety pin and Mama pushed it through our clothes and attached the number to it. The Grønn-Nielsen family was 14364/4, the four at the end indicating that there were four of us in the family. Mama made sure that every time we changed we removed the safety pin and pinned it to the clothes we were wearing. She drummed it into us that we must wear our number every time we went out into the garden.

It was all a big adventure to me. The first morning I was in the church camp at Our Lady, the Virgin Mary, I couldn't wait to explore. I was a little disappointed as I expected the garden area to be bigger. Walking out from our sleeping area, directly in front of me, about thirty metres away, were the showers and sink area, which was covered by a dirty corrugated-iron roof. On one side were the showers and on the other side the sinks, which were separated by a crudely constructed bamboo wall. There were three sinks and three showers and one of the shower cubicles didn't have a door, which meant the Japs could stare at the women as they washed. There always seemed to be someone in the showers. A queue and one or two guards always lingered there.

I walked around the showers towards the walls of the garden when I was hit by the most horrid smell imaginable. There were two toilets behind the shower block, tucked away in the corner of the garden, and a thousand flies buzzed above them. As I approached them I needed to answer a call of nature. I tried to fight it, but the pain just got worse. I joined a queue of about twenty people and covered my nose and mouth, swatting at the flies. Everyone covered their nose and mouth, some with hankies and pieces of rag, others with their bare hands, while some just pinched their noses and breathed through their mouths, flicking at the flies that attempted to land on their lips.

The toilet was just a hole in the ground with two spaces for your feet. You were expected to squat down and do your business and, to make matters worse, there was no running water, so the flies hung on the walls like a moving black carpet. I literally fell from the cubicle as I completed my task and the women outside laughed and told me I'd get used to it.

They were wrong: I never, ever got used to it and every time I had to set foot in one of those cubicles I couldn't get out fast enough. The water supply in the church was always a problem and, although the showers and sinks had taps with running water, the water went off several times every week. When this happened the Japs would bring in a water tanker to fill up the tanks. They would attach a large hose and order the women to clean out the toilets. The flies in the toilet would disappear for a few hours, but then find their way back in again.

I made my way back to the church; it was always quiet in there, almost like a sanctuary. I sat down on my bed and looked at Mama, who was curled up with Lasse. Lasse was fast asleep again and, although Mama's eyes were closed, I could sense she was not sleeping, just resting. Her eyes opened when she heard a beautiful sound. We looked at each other and she smiled. It was a tune I had never heard before, and it reminded me that I had been without the simple pleasure of music for a long time. When was the last time I had heard beautiful music? I remembered: it was in our house at Surabaya as I sat with Papa listening to the radio. The songs and classic tunes were interrupted by the stern voice of the radio man as he told us all about the war in Europe and Africa and, towards the end, the war in the Pacific. The delightful almost perfect-pitch music brought me back from my thoughts. Where was this beautiful tune coming from?

'It's "Lullaby" by Johannes Brahms,' Mama said as she sat up. 'It's so very pretty, isn't it, Lise?'

We looked across at a small boy crouched over something in between his knees. He caressed it as it played its melody. I was really tired, but I had to find out where the tune was coming from, so I walked over to him. He looked up as I reached him and cowered in fright. I put a hand on his shoulder, smiling.

'Please don't tell, don't tell those horrible nasty yellow men,' he said.

'Don't worry,' I replied, 'I won't tell them.'

He smiled. 'My name is Robert,' he whispered. He sat up straight and let me see the small wooden box between his knees and with a proud grin announced, 'And this is my very own music box.'

Robert explained that he had been in Japanese prisoner of war camps for nearly two years and had managed to keep his treasure a secret. It was no bigger than a small cigar box and colourfully painted with patterns of flowers and oriental-looking trees.

We sat for hours playing the same tunes over and over again, but eventually, as darkness came, I returned to Mama and settled down for the night. I fell asleep to the noise that quietly danced around the church and imagined myself in a place far away with an orchestra playing and an elegant bandmaster in fine black clothes, a crisp white shirt and a proud smile on his face. I dreamed that night of nice things: peace and food, good clothes and soft pillows. For once my sleeping thoughts were pleasant ones, not the nightmares I had grown accustomed to.

I would sit with Robert for many nights as he played his music box to me. He would be the conductor in beautiful clothes and I was his audience. Robert became one of my best friends in the church camp and we always had a special bond through our shared love of a few simple tunes.

*

Two days after we arrived at the camp we had our first *tenko*. Nothing had changed.

Mama hurried us up and made sure our cardboard numbers were pinned to our chest. Everyone in the camp was on parade and a Japanese officer instructed two soldiers to count the bodies and make a note of the numbers. The two soldiers started from opposite ends of the long line, scribbling furiously. They met in the middle, added figures and presented them to the officer. The officer was not happy and shouted at them to begin again. We stood for over an hour until eventually the two soldiers got the numbers correct. Mama whispered to me that they were stupid little men who were so uneducated that they couldn't even count right. I laughed at them under my breath; I was only ten years old and yet I could count well past one thousand. I reassured myself yet again that these men could not possibly win the war.

At the end of the first week the soldiers announced at *tenko* that the Japanese Emperor had ordered that the prisoners under his protection had to be fit and healthy. They said that the conditions in the prisoner of war camps and the food given to us were far better than the conditions and food that the enemy was supplying to its prisoners. We listened in amazement as he announced we would be taking gymnastic exercises every morning. The soldier stood in front of the long line with his arms above his head and ordered us to copy his actions as he jumped and bounced and stretched for ten minutes. We children thought it was great fun, but even the sick and weak were made to join in.

Another soldier patrolled the back of the line with his rifle, and if he thought anybody was underperforming they were rewarded with a rifle butt in their back.

After the gymnastics, we queued up for our breakfast, a tasteless, grey porridgy sludge. The cooking facilities were much the same as they had been in the first camp. The food was brought in on lorries and the women unloaded it while the Japanese soldiers stood and watched. The rice and flour came in huge sacks, which the women heaved down two at a time. There were the familiar black cast-iron cooking pots on the lorry, too, containing some sort of food that had steam rising from it. I tried hard to catch an aroma in the air, something tempting, the smell of meat or some sort of spice, but although the steam passed in my direction I could smell nothing. Some of the women climbed up onto the lorry and threaded bamboo poles through the pot handles. Four women took each end of the bamboo pole and lowered them carefully to another four women on the ground. I could see it was a huge effort for the weak and undernourished ladies and I couldn't help but notice the Japanese soldiers looking on and doing nothing to help as they struggled. It was as if the task was beneath them.

The Japs placed great importance on *tenko*, whenever they decided to call it. Although it was generally in the morning, it didn't follow any pattern. Sometimes there would be no *tenko* for a week, at other times it was every day and very occasionally a *tenko* would be called last thing at night. No matter what it was you were doing, *tenko* always came first. Every now and again someone would be caught on the toilet or in the shower and the Japanese officer taking the parade would shout and get very angry.

One morning a young woman had been taking a shower and had not heard the roll call. By the time she stepped from the cubicle we were lined up and the Japanese soldiers were counting us and checking all of the numbers. The girl was only about twenty-two years of age and she panicked, running over to the line dressed only in a towel, which she held to her chest, trying to preserve her modesty. She bowed and apologized to the officer and took her place in the line. She was no more than a minute late. The officer walked over and I could see almost immediately that he was starting to get angry. The one thing I remember about him was his horrible yellow, almost green teeth as he snarled and shouted at the girl. Why? I thought to myself, why is he getting angry? These Japanese soldiers were not in the war fighting in a far-off land; they were looking after a camp in the middle of a small town. It was the same routine, day in, day out. The officer looked down at her towel.

'Where is number?' he shouted.

The poor girl explained she had been in the shower and hadn't had time to collect her clothes.

'Go collect now,' he commanded. The poor girl bowed again and backed away out of the line.

She flew down the garden and into the church. In less than a minute she was back in line with her number pinned to the towel, apologizing again to the officer for disrupting his parade.

The officer looked along the line and took a step back to address us.

'Number very important. At *tenko* always number.'

He stepped forward and unpinned the number from the girl's towel. He held it up so that we could all see.

'More important than anything. Never forget.' He pointed at the girl. 'This girl never forget number again.'

He called the girl forward and she obeyed. The officer still held the cardboard number above his head. He lowered it and unhinged the safety pin still attached to the piece of card. It was no more than three centimetres long and very old. It had rusted with the perspiration of the user over the period she had worn it. He stepped forward and spoke to the parade.

'Girl never forget number again.'

He reached forward and tugged at the girl's tight skin between her breast and collar bone. She was slim and undernourished and he struggled as he attempted to get enough of her flesh between his thumb and forefinger. She winced and caught her breath as he nipped harder. He stood for a few seconds, satisfied that he had gathered enough skin to perform his grisly task. We watched in horror as he took the safety pin and began pushing it into her flesh. She cried out in pain as he punctured her skin. He shouted at her to be quiet. Immediately a flow of blood appeared and poured onto her wet towel. He pulled at the skin even harder as the tears ran down the girl's face. He pushed at the pin, prodding and poking until eventually it burst through the other side and another line of blood oozed from her chest. He manoeuvred the pin back and forth until he was satisfied that enough of it poked through the flesh and, with a smile, he snapped the safety catch closed. The cardboard number blew gently on the breeze as more and more blood poured from the wounds.

I could not tear my eyes away from the girl's towel, which was slowly turning into a psychedelic robe of pain. The poor girl held her hand across her chest and the blood, sweat and tears blended into one. Every few seconds the pattern changed and grew bigger, and I imagined her pain and dismay growing accordingly. I could not believe what I had just seen. I wanted to run to the girl and comfort her. I wanted to take one of the soldiers' bayonets and ram it into the officer's chest. But I could do nothing. I wanted to dig a hole, climb in and sleep through the nightmare I had just witnessed. Some of the ladies and children were crying and I looked in disgust at the officer, who continued delivering his lecture in broken English.

He talked for another ten minutes. By the time he had finished and dismissed the line, the grey-white towel was soaked red. As he walked away the girl collapsed and several ladies went to help her. One of the nuns appeared on the scene and, while several ladies held the crying girl down, she pulled the rusty pin from her chest. The girl gave a loud squeal as it came free and a bigger scream as the nun fed the puncture wounds with iodine. It took all my strength not to join her crying. They pulled her to her feet and she was helped away in the direction of the rooms they called the hospital.

A little while later I spotted the same officer over at the

gateway, laughing and joking with some of the guards. I wondered what kind of man could do that sort of thing to a poor, defenceless woman and show not one ounce of remorse.

The poor girl survived her ordeal, though when I passed her several days later she was not the same person. Gone was the pretty smile and the sparkle in her eyes that I remembered. Mama said she had blood poisoning and a fever for many days. Mama also said that an older lady would not have survived. It was her youth that had pulled her through.

CHAPTER 10

Death of an Angel

I noticed the rope hanging from the ceiling one day as I explored a different part of the church. It seemed so out of place and I couldn't help but wonder where the end of the rope led. It lay on a partition made from bamboo and my curiosity got the better of me as I walked over to it, all the while looking up at the ceiling, where it disappeared into the roof. At the end of the rope that hung over the bamboo was a big knot with loose threads. My mouth fell open as I moved quietly behind the bamboo barrier and saw what was there. It reminded me of the story of Aladdin and the cave where he discovered the treasure. There were gold goblets, silver candelabra and crosses encrusted with red and green jewels. I counted at least ten beautiful crystal glasses, their stems and bases painted gold, and a shiny silver tray with at least thirty holes, each one containing a tiny polished glass that seemed to reflect the light coming through the stained-glass window.

I was aware of Mama standing beside me as if she had appeared from nowhere.

'You should not be here, little one,' she remarked.

'What is it, Mama?' I asked, still staring at the gold, silver and jewels at my feet. 'A secret treasure?'

She nodded. 'Yes, little one, it is the treasure of religion.'

'But why have the Japs not taken it?'

Mama shrugged her shoulders as she placed a hand on top of my head.

'Fear, I suppose.'

'Fear?' I enquired.

'The fear of religion; they are scared to take it in case God strikes them down.' Her eyes looked up at the ceiling. 'Or much, much worse.'

It didn't make any sense. The Japs had confiscated everything during our time in the camps: money, jewellery, even the clothes from people's backs, and yet they had left this hoard of treasure intact? I simply couldn't understand it; I didn't want to understand it. My eyes fixed almost magnetically on the rope again.

'And this, Mama? What is this? Where does it lead?'

I reached out and took hold of the knot at the end of the rope. Mama's hand was swift as she placed it on top of mine.

'Do not touch that bell, my little one, it is very special.' She gently released my hand and placed it by my side before continuing. She looked up into the ceiling.

'The rope is attached to a bell that has not rung for years.'

I shook my head and was just about to speak when she answered the very question I was going to ask.

'It will ring when this terrible war is over. The bell will ring and ring and it will be heard by every boy and girl in the world. It will signal peace and we will be free to walk and talk and smile, eat when we want and sleep in beds with white cotton sheets and soft pillows. It will ring when we are on the ship to Norway and it will still be ringing when we arrive in Bergen and, if it's raining, it will not matter because that bell will ring forever.'

'Let's ring it now, Mama,' I said. 'Let's make the war end.'

Mama smiled.

'It's not that simple, Lisemor. We must be patient.' She gazed at the rope. 'It will ring soon, little one, I promise. The bell will ring soon.' And with that she took my hand and led me away.

The church camp was very boring for the children as there were no toys to play with and schooling was forbidden. Although we had several teachers in the camp, the Japs refused to allow us any education unless it was learning the Japanese language. They were keen enough for us to learn that, but anything else was simply not allowed. After several weeks we were so bored that the teachers decided to teach us secretly behind the closed doors of the church. It was cool in the church and a huge relief from the heat outside. The lessons began to take shape. We took the lessons for several weeks, always after a *tenko* parade when the guards had disappeared for breakfast. We could hear them through the fence, eating and drinking, the cutlery banging off their tin plates. There never seemed to be any shortage of food on the Japanese side of the fence, and some of the beautiful cooking smells that used to drift across the garden of the camp at breakfast time were sheer torture to every starving European prisoner held there.

The guards were never seen for at least an hour after *tenko*, and this was how long the lessons lasted. There were three teachers who took turns: all of them were Dutch ladies, but my favourite was Miss Helena. Miss Helena was from Amsterdam in Holland and she was very pretty. She would draw us pictures of the canals in Amsterdam and tell us about the flower festivals. She had a supply of coloured crayons that we had to return after each lesson, and she would count them one by one to make sure none were missing.

Miss Helena and the other teachers did not dare risk any more than one hour of teaching, but nevertheless it was something that we all looked forward to every day. On Sundays we learned about the Bible, God, Jesus, Mary and Joseph and a man called Moses. It was all very sneaky, but more than a little exciting, too. After *tenko* the children would drift around the garden; some would go to the toilet or take a shower, but all the while we would keep an eye on the guards. Then as soon as the last one had disappeared from the compound we would rush into the church.

Once we entered the church there was a strict code to be obeyed. Miss Helena (or one of the others) would sit in a corner arranging paper, pencils and crayons. She would be in the opposite corner to that of the Japanese office outside the church, sitting on the floor, almost hidden from view by the rows of benches where we slept at night. We would creep in silently, telling the younger children to stop giggling, and the lesson would be conducted in a series of whispers. I think the secrecy added to the excitement of each lesson.

The lessons came to an end all too soon, but afterwards I would seek out Miss Helena in the garden and she was only too happy to answer more questions about the lessons, particularly questions about Holland and Norway. She had an incredible knowledge of European countries and told me she had visited the fjords and been to Paris and London.

One day we were having a lesson on England when the Japanese guards burst through the doors on the opposite side of the church. We had drawn the shape of the map of the British Isles, and had separated the outline into the countries of Scotland, England, Ireland and Wales. I was beginning to colour in Wales with a deep-red crayon when I heard a commotion behind me. The guards were running along the back of the church towards us. Miss Helena was desperately trying to gather up the pencils and paper and instinctively I dived under the benches to get out of the way. I lay cowering on the floor, watching those horrible black boots kicking out at the children who had not managed to get out of the way, stamping on the crayons and pencils. I screwed my eyes tight shut and covered my ears. When I opened my eyes, I could see the shape of Miss Helena being dragged along the floor towards the door to the garden. She was crying and her face was covered in blood. I lay under the benches until the guards had gone. Almost immediately the cry of *tenko* came from outside.

I caught up with Mama in the garden as we rushed towards the line that was beginning to form. Mama checked that we all had our numbers attached and we took our place on parade. Miss Helena was not in the line; she was standing between two Japs who were facing us. After a short delay a Japanese officer turned up. I watched my dear teacher's face as he approached us. She looked very, very frightened as the blood mixed with her tears.

'Prisoner not follow orders,' he boomed in a voice that almost shook the foundations of the church.

'No school,' he continued. 'Only school in Japanese. Prisoner must be punished.'

He nodded at one of the guards. The man took a step forward and raised his rifle high into the air. With all his strength he hammered it into the side of Miss Helena's head. The side of her face split open and she immediately fell to the floor. A pool of blood formed on the ground and the sight of it caused one of the ladies to faint. Women around me were crying and the children who had been at Miss Helena's school only a few minutes before buried their faces in their mothers' clothing.

I watched.

I looked on in utter disbelief, but I kept watching because I wanted Miss Helena to stand and because I wanted it to be over. Incredibly I noticed a slight movement in my teacher's eyes. The officer noticed it, too, and signalled once again to the soldiers, who helped her to her feet. She was very wobbly but eventually the soldiers stood back when she was able to stand on her own. She held the side of her head as the blood seeped from between her fingers. I don't think I could ever have imagined that much blood coming from such a wound. It covered her blouse and her skirt and fell in drops onto the dry earth.

I couldn't believe the blow to her head had not killed her, but she stood still and, although she was crying, I could see she was getting stronger by the second.

The Japanese officer nodded his head to one of the soldiers, who repeatedly and viciously attacked her with his rifle until she collapsed in a heap once again. I made an attempt to run forward and tell them to stop, but Mama hugged me tight around the shoulders and refused to let me go. Then the other soldier joined in with his boot. I covered my eyes but could not block out the noise. The sounds of the two soldiers kicking and hitting her went on and on and, although I had nothing in my stomach, I felt sick. They beat her for a full minute; they beat her until she moved no more. I uncovered my eyes . . . They had beaten her to a pulp; she didn't stir. By now the line of women and children were hysterical; the screams and shouts echoed around the compound as the guards dragged Miss Helena away.

The officer delivered a lecture about obedience and punishment, then dismissed us.

The Japs threw Miss Helena into one of the small rooms at the side of the church. I do not know what the rooms were used for, but I had noticed them before. They had no windows and were not big enough for a bed. Mama said they were storage rooms.

The Japanese officer told the ladies that Miss Helena should have four days of punishment. She was to receive no food or water and no medical treatment. She was locked inside. The Japanese officer placed the key in his pocket and walked away. A guard had been placed on the outside of the church building only a few metres from where poor Miss Helena lay in her dark room. He sat on a mat right outside the entrance to check that no one went near her or gave her food and water.

The first night was the worst: I could hear Miss Helena moaning; just moaning, nothing else. The sound echoed around the still church. Her moaning came every twenty minutes or so, followed by the gentle crying of one of the ladies who could bear no more.

After a few hours the moaning stopped. I prayed she had simply fallen asleep. The following day I walked from my bed and stood by the doorway where Miss Helena lay. I told her I was there. I told her the door was locked and I couldn't help her. She didn't reply and I ran away before I burst into tears.

I begged Mama to help her and she said she would try. Mama called a meeting but wouldn't let me listen. She said afterwards that one of the women could get into the room using a nail file and some wire so that she would get some food and water to Miss Helena during the hours of darkness. She mentioned that one of the other ladies would distract the guard.

The women were as true as their word and I lay awake, watching through the corner of my eye as a silhouette fiddled quietly with the lock. Please hurry, I whispered to myself under my breath, scared that the Japs would discover her. At last, after what seemed like an eternity, the door opened and she pushed some water and a bowl of porridge in before relocking it and quickly returning to her bed.

I couldn't sleep for worrying about my favourite teacher.

A few hours later the lady returned and opened the door again, much quicker this time, and took the bowls away.

I couldn't see, but I prayed that the bowls she had taken away had been emptied. The following night they repeated the exercise and, despite being exhausted, I fought sleep and managed to stay awake, trying to catch a glimpse of Miss Helena.

I never saw her.

On the third morning at *tenko*, the Japanese officer announced that my teacher's door would be opened. I looked along the line and the boys and girls were smiling. I looked at the adults, but strangely they all looked quite serious. Before the ladies went into the church the Japanese soldiers walked away. I thought this was odd. Didn't they want to see Miss Helena?

All the children gathered outside the church, excited that our teacher was being let out. The Japanese had given the key to one of the nuns and she walked in with Mama and a few of the other ladies. They walked into the church with a bottle of water, some bread and a banana. I imagined Miss Helena walking out smiling, like a long-lost aunt returning home. I imagined her munching on the banana; I imagined her wounds and bruises to have disappeared; I imagined her like she was . . . my favourite teacher.

I waited and waited.

I wanted to walk to the door of the room, but Mama had given me strict instructions to stay outside.

Mama and the other ladies were in the church for an age. Eventually Mama walked out.

Something was wrong. Mama was crying, wiping at the tears running down her cheek. Behind her the nun was crying, too.

'What's happened?' I asked. 'Where is she, where is Miss Helena?'

Mama took my hand and turned me away from the church.

'I'm sorry, Lisemor,' she said. 'Your teacher is dead.'

CHAPTER 11

Sugar for Flies

~❧~

It saddens me to say so, but I got over the horrible ordeal of seeing my teacher beaten to death by pushing the incident into the distant reaches of my mind and trying to pretend it hadn't happened. Although never a day goes by when the image of that brutal beating does not come into my head, within a few days I was laughing and playing with my friends. I began to have huge feelings of guilt every time I laughed. I began to get annoyed with the other children too when they laughed, thinking to myself, why are they laughing? I even got annoyed with Robert when he played his music box, even though the tunes soothed me. Didn't they realize poor Miss Helena was dead? But as the days passed, slowly the thoughts became easier to manage and forget about, and I dared to imagine that the many beatings and acts of brutality I had witnessed over the months I had been imprisoned were in fact normal . . . part of everyday life. I hadn't ever heard of the word at the time, but I was becoming 'desensitized', in much the same way a soldier does during war. The first shooting or killing is the worst . . . thereafter it gets easier. I had seen many beatings, including the disgusting act the Japanese officer had carried out on the girl who had forgotten her number on parade, and now I had witnessed my dear, special friend Miss Helena being beaten half to death before being thrown into a room to die.

It was during the hours of darkness that the nightmare images resurfaced and refused to go away. I lay awake in tears on many nights, wondering when was the precise moment that she died. Mama and the ladies never mentioned her again, as if somehow not talking about her would erase the memories from the children's minds. I'd heard her moaning for a few nights, I was sure of it, and as much as I wanted to believe she hadn't suffered in that dark hole the Japanese had thrown her into, there was no doubt in my mind that she had suffered more than I could imagine. I asked myself the question over and over again. Why?

The flies in the camp were like a plague of locusts, particularly near the toilets and anywhere there was food. At times I looked down into my bowl of rice and there seemed to be more flies than grains. Most of the children were developing pus-filled sores and blisters, which the flies homed in on. It seemed the only time we were at peace from the flies was at night, when we draped our wooden benches with mosquito nets. So it was inevitable that the vast majority of the camp came down with illnesses and fevers, and dysentery was commonplace.

It seemed that every day at least one or two of the mothers would simply disappear. It was a familiar pattern: the mothers would give portions, and sometimes all of their rations, to their children. The older ladies at the camp instructed the children not to take their mothers' rations and begged us to refuse anything offered to us. We were all very hungry, so it was very difficult, but for some of the children it was nigh on impossible and they took anything that was offered. The mothers grew weaker and weaker and when they came down with a virus or a fever, their system could not fight it. I watched them lie still; I watched the colour drain from their faces and their skeletons showing through their wasted flesh.

And then they were gone.

I asked Mama where they had gone, but she never answered.

Those flies, those horrible flies that flew down the toilets, then onto our bread and rice. I blamed the flies for everything.

The flies had two favourite spots in the camp: the toilets and the rubbish dump over by the gate at the very top corner of the garden. The rubbish would be piled up by a truck and every few days the Japs would order some of the ladies to load it, after which it was driven away to be dumped.

There was also a wooden handcart by the truck with a huge brown tarpaulin covering it. There were many different opin-ions as to what was under that tarpaulin, some of them quite ridiculous, but over the days, whatever was underneath there grew bigger and bigger and then eventually the guards would open the gates and let some ladies wheel it out. As soon as the cart was moved, thousands of flies would fly out from underneath the tarpaulin and the guards would shout and scream, swatting them away with their hats. When it returned the tarpaulin was flat against the bottom of the cart and the flies had gone.

One of the Dutch ladies, Mrs Haas, announced after parade that she had had enough of the bloody flies and she was going to do something about it. Mama and some of the other ladies begged her not to but, determined as she was, she knocked on the door of the gate, and when a soldier opened it she demanded to see the officer in charge. This was simply not done; nobody demanded to see any Japanese.

She argued with the guard for a little while and he slammed the door shut. Part of me was relieved; hopefully the guard would not bother the officer and it would be forgotten.

It was not to be.

A few minutes later the gate was opened and a Japanese officer strolled through with his hands behind his back. I could not take my eyes off the huge sword that hung from his belt. As he walked into the compound, Mrs Haas approached him, bowing as she walked. He ordered her to stop and they spoke to each other, but I could not make out what they were saying. The Japanese officer turned around and walked towards the gate. He stopped and beckoned Mrs Haas to follow him. As the gate closed behind them my heart was in my mouth. I was convinced I would never see her again.

It was the longest fifteen minutes of my life, but miraculously Mrs Haas returned with a smile on her face. Smiles were rare in the church compound, even on the faces of the children, so everyone in the camp seemed to sit up and take notice.

Mrs Haas called a meeting and made all the children sit in front of her. The mothers stood behind us, ever curious to know what it was she was so happy about.

Mrs Haas said she had explained the problem of the flies to the Japanese officer and about the disease and problems they were causing. She said he had been very understanding and agreed that it was affecting the Japanese guards, too, as at least four of them were confined to sick bay. The Japanese officer said that it was very important that all prisoners of the Emperor remained fit and well. As Mrs Haas continued, she looked at all the children and smiled.

'So we are going to start a new game today. The game is called fly hunt.'

She explained that this new game would carry a reward for the children who caught the most flies. As we sat with our mouths open, Mrs Haas disclosed that the Japanese officer had agreed that, for every one hundred flies killed and presented to him, he would give a teaspoon of sugar.

Sugar!

I had forgotten what sugar tasted like. It had been so long. I recalled Mama sprinkling sugar on strawberries and mangoes and sometimes even bread. I remembered her baking in our beautiful kitchen in Surabaya and the smell and taste of the biscuits and cakes she made. I remembered the sugar being tipped into the bowl and sometimes sprinkled on top; waiting forever until the cakes and biscuits came out of the oven, and waiting even longer until they cooled down enough so that they wouldn't burn our mouths.

Sugar . . .

One hundred flies and we would be given a teaspoon of sugar. At first I thought a hundred flies seemed an awful lot but I soon realized my mind had blocked out the almost constant buzzing of the little pests.

They were everywhere.

I looked around in the air, on the walls, in the dirt, on our clothes, our hair and our skin and I realized there were millions of them.

We set to work immediately. Every child in the compound took on the challenge. We improvised with makeshift fly swats. Sticks were gathered from the garden area and attached to pieces of cardboard by making two small holes and threading the sticks through them. We tried to make the cardboard swats bigger to hit more flies, but soon realized that they didn't travel through the air so quickly so the flies could escape. If they were too little it was easy to miss. We settled on the perfect size – ten centimetres across – and experimented by puncturing the card with hundreds of little holes so the air could pass through more easily. By the end of the first day we had perfected our fly swats.

There was no escape for those dirty little creatures. We killed flies everywhere, starting with the toilet area and actually fighting with each other to see who could get the best spot. By the end of the day children were counting up their booty, ready to present it to the ladies' committee. I shared my catch with Karin, even though I killed more than her. We placed them on a piece of cardboard in rows of ten to make the counting easier. We had killed two hundred and seventy-six between us that first day. We were twenty-four short of the three hundred, but the following morning at the crack of dawn, before *tenko*, armed with our fly swats we went hunting. It was so early the flies weren't even out of bed, but gradually they began to surface. It was hard work, but we made up just enough to qualify for three teaspoons of sugar.

By the end of the week there was hardly a fly to be seen anywhere, and it took us much longer to collect a hundred flies after that. The exercise had worked. Mrs Haas was very proud that she had managed to rid the camp of flies and we children were more than pleased that we had a game to relieve the boredom – and a game that gave us extra sugar.

At the end of the week the Japs brought in a huge bag of sugar and it was lifted onto one of the kitchen tables. We stood in a big line with our flies, which we tipped onto a piece of cardboard. Every fly was counted meticulously by the ladies. They used two strips of cardboard to move the flies as they didn't want to touch them. We stood patiently until it was announced how many spoonfuls of sugar we had qualified for. We then moved to another lady, who tipped the exact number of spoonfuls into our battered white enamel cups.

It was like Christmas all over again. Sugar . . . we had sugar!

Afterwards the flies were burned in a ceremonial-type bonfire in a huge wok with holes in. The nuns told us it was to prevent disease as flies were the dirtiest creatures on God's planet. We children looked upon it as a kind of celebration, ridding our camp of pests and of course receiving sugar as a reward. I'll never forget the smell from the burning-fly smoke; I covered my nose and mouth instinctively, convincing myself that if I breathed in the noxious substance I would suffer a fate worse than death. As the tiny bodies of the flies popped and cracked in the flames the children shouted, cheered and danced a jig of joy. The commandant came by occasionally and watched over proceedings. Although he never showed much emotion, he seemed pleased with our work. I noticed he didn't seem so angry. Mrs Haas said he was very pleased.

Every evening, after the fire had died down, we went straight to Mama as instructed, but not before we had licked our fingers and dipped them in the sugar several times. Mama placed the remaining sugar in a tin and announced that it would be used the next time we had an extra banana.

I looked on with envy for three days as Lasse ate his daily banana. As always, Karin and I got the skins and scraped off what we could with our teaspoons. But then, after a few days, Karin and I were presented with a banana one morning after parade. We ran back to Mama for our banana surprise.

There we mashed the bananas very finely on our plates before adding a little sugar and whipping the mixture until it was nice and fluffy.

Our mouths became moist in anticipation of the taste. Then we were allowed one teaspoon at a time. Karin was first and I watched as the spoon entered her mouth and the expression on her face was one of sheer joy. Lasse was next, then me. It was wonderful. I had become so used to tasteless porridge and rice. It was as if my mouth had exploded, the flavours bursting inside. The sensation was incredible and we were all smiling and groaning in pleasure, making mumbling noises to each other and laughing. I made sure Mama took a spoonful, too, and then we started again with another spoonful. We got three spoonfuls each before it ran out and the last half-spoonful we gave to Lasse, then we let him lick the plate. It was a very special moment and a big boost to us to know that by working on the fly hunt we could get a treat now and again. We also saved some sugar for the tasteless porridge we received most mornings.

I was thankful for being so healthy and strong, despite the appalling conditions, and pleased that I was able to provide a little extra something for my family. Even those nasty flies seemed to serve a useful purpose in the squalid, dirty, starving environment of the camp.

CHAPTER 12

To Catch a Thief

Looking back on my time in the camp, the two things that preyed on my mind most were boredom and, of course, hunger.

There was never enough food to eat, so once again I took to pilfering what I could, when I could. By this time Mama was very slow because of the stiffness in her joints and she was never first in the queue when the food was dished out. Sometimes she was so wracked with pain that she could not manage to stand in the queue long enough for the rations to be handed out. I think there were over twelve hundred women and children in the church camp and, even though the rations were divided out as small as possible, at least twenty or thirty people every day got nothing at all.

I tried to explain to the ladies dishing out food that Mama was sick and could not make it to the queue, asking them if I could have two lots of rations, but they would not allow it. Rules were rules, they said, and if Mama wanted food she would have to make the effort. That's when I started to fill my pockets with anything I could take from the tables. I pinched scraps of bread, I pulled out a handful of rice from my bowl and pushed it into my pocket whenever the dinner lady wasn't looking, then stood still looking innocently at my empty bowl. The lady would get confused and look at me suspiciously. I would open my mouth and show her it was empty and she would have no choice but to give me more.

Bananas were my prize catch, especially when we had a reserve supply of sugar. Any child under two got a banana every day and I knew there were more than enough to go round. The older children would get a banana only occasionally and I'm sure the rest went to the ladies who served the food. A banana was easy to pinch, but not so easy to hide. I devised a plan where I would tuck the waistband of my shorts into the front of my knickers to catch anything that might find its way down the front of my blouse. As I passed the pile of bananas, I simply flicked one down the front of my blouse. The banana would fall down and rest on the waistband. I was very cunning and no one ever suspected or caught me. If I thought there were too many people looking in my direction then I would simply leave my pilfering until the next day.

I was getting good at finding scraps of food and managed to build up a little bit of a larder in my rucksack, just in case things changed. Occasionally a delivery didn't arrive and we went hungry. I was also very aware that the Japs could move us at any time and I thought back to that awful march from the station with no food and water.

I felt very smart as I lay down to sleep that night. Although we were still a little hungry, we weren't uncomfortably so. In my rucksack, in a small tin, I had a piece of bread, a portion of burned rice, which we called kra, and, more precious than anything, a beautiful ripe banana in the bottom. I would share the banana with my family after tomorrow's awful breakfast of porridge, which I could barely eat without throwing up. It had no taste and Mama said it was just like eating glue. Yes, tomorrow I would surprise my family. We would fill our stomachs with porridge and enjoy the treat of the banana afterwards.

I hadn't been asleep for very long when I awoke with a start. It was still pitch-black but I was aware of shouting and the beams of torches penetrating the darkness. I heard calls of *tenko, tenko*. This was unusual; what were the Japs doing? Mama told me there was an inspection and we climbed out of bed as quickly as we could. Some of the younger children were crying because they were frightened and some of the weaker women struggled to make it to their feet after being woken so suddenly. We were lined up in the church and the Japanese ordered us to bring our bags with us. Five soldiers searched every bag in the pile in front of us and took everything they could find.

They took money – Malayan currency and Dutch guilders – jewellery and items of clothing and, right there in front of us, they destroyed any food they found. I watched in horror as a soldier picked up my rucksack and tipped it on the floor. He grabbed the tin where I had stored the bread and burned rice, tipped it on the floor and stamped on it with his dirty boot. He then reached into my bag again and found my banana. He threw it down onto the growing food pile and, with a grin, twisted his foot back and forth until the mixture blended into one horrible, sludgy mess.

I felt like screaming; I had worked so hard to keep a little food back for emergencies or luxuries and yet again I questioned the mentality and sheer evil cruelty of the Japanese. The officer had said the Emperor of Japan wanted his prisoners to be healthy, so why were they destroying perfectly good food when it was so scarce? Some of the ladies were crying now as one by one every single bag and container was searched ruthlessly and anything edible was stamped into the dirty wooden floor of the church.

But the worst was yet to come.

Out of the corner of my eye I spotted Robert. He looked absolutely terrified and his eyes were locked in a stare. I followed his gaze and looked in horror at the focus of his attention. A Japanese guard held the music box up into the beam of his colleague's torch, not quite sure what it was he had unearthed. He fiddled with the brass clasp on the box and the lid opened. The moment seemed to freeze in time as the familiar tune permeated the cool night air. A few of the soldiers paused for a second, not quite sure where the sound was coming from. Some of the ladies looked up in bewilderment and young Robert actually smiled. The look was infectious and, despite my fear and disgust at what the Japanese were doing, I felt my face break into a cautious grin.

The Jap guard sneered, threw the box into the middle of the food pile and crushed it with his boot. The little box let out a few desperate last notes and died there and then.

Ten minutes later the guards were gone.

I wanted to go over to Robert and put my arms around him to console him – he was my best friend – but when I looked into his eyes I knew it would do no good. He walked away, crawled onto his bed and curled up in a ball, oblivious to everything going on around him. I shed a tear for him when his little body shook and trembled as his heart broke.

Other people were crying and desperately trying to retrieve scraps of food from the pile in the middle of the floor. The broken bits of wood and clockwork were thrown to one side and I thought for a second about retrieving them. It was no good, though: they were smashed and bent and twisted and broken beyond repair. Nevertheless, I collected what I could and placed the bits in the bottom of my rucksack. When the time was right I would give them back to Robert.

We hadn't noticed in the darkness, but one of the ladies had not made the parade in the church. She was so weak she had simply lain still and hoped that the Japs would not notice her. Her skeletal figure had simply blended in with the blankets. It wasn't until we returned to bed that I noticed her and told Mama.

'That is Mrs Muhren,' she said. 'She is not well.'

Mama knelt down where Mrs Muhren lay and dabbed at her head with a handkerchief. Even in the darkness I could make out the beads of sweat on her forehead. Her eyes were like hollow sunken holes in her head and her face showed no emotion whatsoever: no pain, no pity, no hope.

The following evening her bed space was empty and her only

boy wandered about in a daze before one of the other women took him into bed beside her.

'Where has Mrs Muhren gone?' I asked Mama.

'Hospital,' she said.

Several days passed and Mrs Muhren did not return. In the end I stopped asking.

The rumours persisted about what was under the tarpaulin on the handcart that stood between the rubbish dump and the truck by the gate. By now the fly problem in the camp had almost been eradicated and qualifying for an extra spoonful of sugar was becoming more and more difficult. I had been hunting with Karin the whole morning when eventually she gave up and went back into the church to see Mama and Lasse.

I noticed the handcart was swarming with flies. I looked around the compound at the other children, who were on the prowl looking for the tiny flies that could yield so much sweet treasure. I settled down, placed my cardboard swat on the ground and my collection of flies on top.

Twenty-six.

We had hunted the whole morning and killed only twenty-six flies. I would never get a spoonful of sugar at this rate. Unless . . .

I looked over at the rubbish dump again and the handcart was absolutely swarming with the creatures. Why did the children not go there? Yes, their mamas had warned them to stay away, but why? Mama had told Karin and me to stay away a dozen times, but she had not said why.

Every few days some of the ladies were told to move the cart. They went over with spades and shovels that the Japanese had issued them with and only the strong were chosen for the task. They disappeared out of the compound for a few hours. I remember watching them on their return. No expression, no emotion, some were even in tears.

I waited until mid-afternoon. Then the guards disappeared for lunch and most of the prisoners went into the church and dormitories to escape the scorching heat of the sun.

It was just me and the flies.

I made my way over with a big paper bag, making sure no one was out, no one was looking. I needed that sugar, my family needed that sugar. I walked over to the handcart. It was positively covered with sugar – not flies, sugar! I covered my face with my shirtsleeve; the smell was a hundred times worse than it was in the compound.

The first swish of my fly swat connected with the tarpaulin. Four flies lay dead. Four! I had killed four flies with my first attack; this was going to be so easy. They were huge flies, bigger than normal, like huge cockroaches; I even wondered if I would get any extra sugar bringing back flies this size! I waited patiently until they had settled again and swung my swat through the air. It yielded the same result time and time again. I was killing flies in threes, fours, even fives. I swatted and swatted the tarpaulin over and over again, not bothering to collect the flies. I would wait until I had finished. The dead flies lay in piles around the edge of the tarpaulin and on the ground. I swatted for at least an hour and when my body could take no more I sank in a heap on the dusty ground, breathing hard as the beads of sweat dripped from my nose and chin.

I smiled as I surveyed the damage.

I took out my paper bag and starting scooping at the piles of dead flies. There were at least three hundred just on the ground, I estimated, even more on the tarpaulin. It was so easy. The bag was already half full by the time I started on the tarpaulin. I scraped from the top, making four big piles at each corner. The bag was full when I finished; I even had to push down on the flies to fold the top over. I couldn't wait to show Mama and Karin. I decided I would let Karin count them as a reward for her efforts in the morning.

I was so excited and just about ready to run off when my curiosity got the better of me. Monsters, dead bodies, ghosts and vampires were just some of the things the children had said were under this dirty tarpaulin. I looked around carefully. There was no one around. I would take a little peek and settle the discussions once and for all.

I didn't know why I was trembling as I took a gentle hold of one corner. Was it fear? Excitement? Perhaps a mixture of both. I bent my head to the level of the cart and lifted gently. A swarm of flies flew from underneath and I closed my eyes quickly as they went past my head. I opened my eyes and stared at the maggot-filled eye sockets of a dead body. I was staring at the face of Mrs Muhren.

Behind her, piled up naked, were more dead women and even

a small boy no more than three years old. Then the smell hit me: the smell of death. My stomach began heaving and I sank to my knees as I began to make sense of it all. I vomited into the dust and began to tremble and shake. The women were not disappearing or going into hospital: they were dying, slowly starving to death. Now I knew why the ladies carried spades and shovels. And the one thought on my mind as I walked towards the church and sobbed out loud was, when would it be Mama's turn to take her place on the handcart?

I composed myself as best I could. I tried to think of the hundreds of flies and the extra sugar they would yield, and I started to think Mama would be just fine. I would make sure that all of my family survived. Even if I had to go back to that tarpaulin and handcart full of dead bodies, my family would be just fine. I would make sure that my family would survive any way I could.

CHAPTER 13

Breaking Bread with the Rats

❧❧❧

When I presented my huge catch of flies to Mama she guessed straightaway where I had collected them from. I expected a scolding, a lecture, but she simply told me to watch out for the rats as they were very dangerous. I had seen the rats around the toilet block and over in the rubbish area and Mama did not need to worry as I was petrified of the horrible long-tailed things. I returned to the handcart many times to kill and collect the flies, which were getting fewer by the day. I now knew exactly what was under the tarpaulin, but I tried to block out my thoughts as I swatted away and imagined my reward at the end of each day. I'd told every child in the camp what was under the dirty brown tarpaulin, and I'm pleased to say only a few brave souls ventured over to add to their dead fly collection.

As the flies almost disappeared, the rat and mouse population seemed to increase. The tiny animals were now so used to sharing their environment with humans, they became braver by the day and more desperate for the scraps and crumbs of food around the compound. It was not unusual to see a mouse run across a table or bench top. At first we jumped and screamed and cursed, but eventually we got used to it.

One day, as the children left the table and one by one the cook-house women drifted away, I spotted half a stick of bread on the back of a shelf. It had obviously been missed. I couldn't quite believe my luck and waited patiently until everyone had gone. I pushed a box over to the shelf and climbed up so that my eye level was the same height as the shelf, then I reached out and took the end of the bread. I became aware of a slight movement in the corner of the shelf and a little resistance. I strained my eyes to see exactly what it was that appeared to be preventing me from taking the bread from the shelf. As I pulled the bread it seemed to pull back to its original position. I gave a sharp tug and the bread broke free. I assumed it had been wedged into the shelf, but as I looked at the place where the bread had been, I came face to face with a huge black rat. It froze in terror. I froze in terror as it bared its horrible, slimy yellow teeth.

Bits of bread hung from its whiskers. I had been performing a bizarre tug of war with a rat. I edged away slowly, scared that any sudden movement might cause the creature to strike out. I climbed down and replaced the box. I looked at the end of the bread that had been gnawed away. I remembered what Mama had told me about the horrid diseases that rats carried, diseases that could kill you, and suddenly the bread didn't seem so appealing, though I wasn't going to give it up that easily. I had won it fair and square. I took a knife from the kitchen and cut away the piece that had been chewed, then I placed the bread in my pocket and ran back to the church as a shiver ran the length of my spine.

The Japanese officer made the announcement at *tenko*. He was very pleased that the fly problem had been brought under control, but now we had to concentrate on the rats and mice. The sugar rewards were revalued with a spoonful of sugar for each mouse caught and two for each rat. The children were fairly desperate for sugar as the flies had all but disappeared, so they set about their task with equal enthusiasm.

The mothers were not very happy that the children were being asked to hunt for rats, but they could not stop the older boys taking up the challenge. All sorts of traps were devised and there were many methods used to kill the creatures once they had been cornered or trapped. I left the rat killing to the older boys as I could not face the horrible creatures. Mama frightened me, too, by explaining that I could easily die if a rat bit me. I thought back to my tug of war with the rat and how near his horrible mouth had been to my fingers. The rats also reminded me of the Japanese soldiers: nasty sharp yellow teeth, black greasy hair and dark evil-looking eyes. Just as I could not confront a Japanese soldier, nor could I confront a rat, not even for two spoonfuls of sugar.

It was during this time that the monsoon rains came, bringing about the greatest rat hunt ever. The rain was relentless and came down in torrents. Everyone watched in fascination from the steps of the church as the gardens of the compound gradually filled with water, creating a huge natural lake.

It was when the water was about half a metre deep that the first rat was spotted swimming out of the toilet block. One of the older boys screamed out in delight and ran back into the church. He came back seconds later stripped to the waist and holding a big stick. Before we knew it he was running through the water holding the stick high above his head. The rat was swimming around in circles, desperately looking for a piece of high ground to climb up on. The boy brought the stick crashing down on the rat's head and it bobbed below the surface before appearing once again, motionless. The boy swung his stick again, just to make sure, then lifted his kill by the tail as he walked back over to the church with a proud grin on his face.

He had no sooner laid the rat on the steps than a second cry went up as another rat was spotted swimming in the rainwater. Two more boys armed themselves with sticks, and within a minute the rat lay dead in the water. The hunt went on for hours, but I think the boys were a little disappointed at the numbers killed. They would watch for what seemed like forever, but no more than six or seven rats made it into the water. Those that did decide to take to the water were all killed. They were slow and cumbersome and stood no chance of escape. By the time darkness came the rain had stopped and everyone gave up watching, realizing that the water was subsiding and every rat had been flushed out and killed. That night the rats' bodies were collected by the women and the sugar was distributed. The ladies said the rats would be burned on a bonfire the following night.

I think I smelled the rats burning, though I could not see where the fire was. I couldn't help noticing that the smell was quite pleasant: burning meat, not unlike a chicken roasting in our oven back home in Surabaya.

In the cabbage soup a few evenings later little flecks of meat appeared and one lady walked round proudly showing off a stringy piece of meat in her soup cup. When I asked one of the ladies serving the soup what it was, she explained that the Japs had brought some chickens into the compound by way of a reward for ridding the camp of all the rats. It flavoured the soup quite nicely and tasted chewy, just like I remembered the texture of chicken back home. I hurried to fetch Mama so that she would not miss out on this unusual occurrence. When I told her that we were having stew tonight, not just cabbage soup, and explained that we were having real meat to eat, she politely declined and went back into the church. Mama said that for once she wasn't very hungry.

It was the first enjoyable sound I had heard since poor Robert had last opened the lid of his music box. The camp was always filled with the sounds of the Japs shouting and yelling, groans from the beds in the church, ladies and children sick and dying, but this was different: it was a noise I was not used to and it was pleasant to the ear. The rainwater had subsided and the sun was shining as a kind of steam lifted into the air like smoke. I couldn't quite see to the far side of the garden where the noise was coming from, but as I walked over I could see the boy sitting beneath the wall, sheltering in the shade. He smiled as I approached him. It was the Dutch boy known as Jaap.

'They're my bamboo clickers,' he said proudly. 'I made them.'

He held two highly polished bamboo sticks between his forefinger and thumb and rattled them against each other. As they came together he moved his hand and wrist and miraculously bashed out a rhythm that echoed round the garden. He sat with another boy who looked a little scared. Jaap introduced him as Arnie from Australia. I sat down beside him and asked what was wrong. He shook his head and smiled.

'Nothing,' he said, 'but I have something very special in here. It's my secret.'

He looked around again and, making sure there were no prying eyes or 'Nips' nearby, he reached into his pocket and pulled out a small wooden harmonica, which he placed to his lips. We had real music. I sat with the boys, who had clearly practised a lot. The melody from the harmonica blended perfectly with the beat from the home-made wooden percussion instrument, and I thought how wonderful it was that such a sound could come out of a place like this. I sat enthralled as the two boys played on and tried hard not to laugh at Jaap, who played his clickers with such concentration that his tongue protruded from the side of his mouth. Later, they advanced to rattling clickers in both hands at the same time.

I wanted to be a part of the camp orchestra.

The bamboo sticks were easy to find as they lay all over the ground of the compound. Shaping and polishing the sticks was the hard bit. We carved out the shapes with knives 'borrowed' from the kitchen. We scorched the sticks in the fires under the cooking pots, polished them with fine sand and then started all over again. Every set of clickers, as we called them, had a different sound, depending on the shape and length and how much they had been polished. Within a few weeks we had a small orchestra and we practised for hours each day. Strangely enough, the Japs didn't seem to mind and eventually even Arnie didn't try to hide his harmonica. For once we had found a pastime that agreed with our captors and they left us alone. It broke the monotony of the day. I began to realize that the Japs were probably as bored with life in the camp as we were.

So we survived . . . barely.

CHAPTER 14

Beriberi, Yellow Fever and Malaria

~~❧~~

By now my ribs were visibly sticking through my chest and when Karin took her shirt off at nights she looked the same. We were always hungry, always, but we begged and scavenged and stole and hunted for flies and mice that would give us some precious life-saving extras. I made sure Mama had her fill and insisted she share in our sugar surprises or the extra banana we were given if the sugar had run out. When we weren't hunting and scavenging for food, we played with the other children, made our music or sat around the compound feeling physically exhausted every night. Sleep came quickly and we didn't have time to worry about the empty feelings in our bellies. Perhaps it was just my imagination, but the rations seemed to be getting smaller.

Mama's legs were very swollen and she spent most of the day lying in bed. Some of the ladies would check on her and occasionally she would be taken away to the hospital for treatment.

The ladies said she had a disease called beriberi and that she needed to be fed more vitamins.

The violence continued. Whenever the Japs called *tenko*, there was a fear that someone had done something wrong and was about to be punished. It was always the same routine: the officer shouting out his displeasure in broken English and a poor woman standing beside him, knowing that, at the very least, a beating was about to begin.

The lady this time was English, a beautiful girl called Margaret. Margaret had two little girls and a boy called Thomas. Thomas was only four years old and had a disease called diabetes. Margaret needed medicine for him and had been caught trying desperately to bribe a guard with a bracelet. She had no money and thought that the guard would take the piece of jewellery as a present for his wife or girlfriend back home. The officer said she had offended the guard, the Japanese nation and also the Emperor. The guard had taken the bracelet and gone straight to the officer with the evidence. The officer called out for the lady's children and they shuffled forward hesitantly. The woman threw herself at the feet of the officer, begging him not to punish the children. The officer ignored her and beckoned for the children to stand in line.

'Whole family to be punished,' he announced. This was unusual as generally children weren't punished. Even if a child was caught stealing it was always the mother who would be beaten.

Margaret beat on the ground in front of him. 'Please, no, no, I will do anything. Punish me,' she cried.

I looked at the three children, who stood there petrified. The oldest girl was no more than seven years old, about the same age as Karin. The officer gave a signal to the guards and they stepped forward with their bayonets pointing at the family. For one horrible second I thought they were about to be killed right there and then. It was not to be. One guard pulled Margaret up by the hair and proceeded to kick her, shouting and pointing at the church. The other guard shepherded her children behind her, slapping them every so often on the backs of their heads. By now the children were in hysterics. The louder they cried, the more the guard hit them. They were instructed to collect their belongings and disappeared inside the church. The officer announced that the whole family would be locked away in the punishment room for five days with only a bowl of porridge in the morning and a cup of water each night. We were ordered to bow once more and then he dismissed us.

The stifled crying of Thomas and his sisters echoed around the church when we retired for the evening. Margaret and her children had been forced into one of the bigger storage cupboards, which was no more than two metres square. I could only imagine the horror behind that dark wooden door. After the first evening there was no sound, no crying, no begging. I couldn't even hear them breathe. The silence was the worst. Why couldn't they sob a little, then at least I'd know they were still alive? I would lie awake when the church was at its most quiet in the early hours of the morning and strain hard to try to imagine a noise, any noise, coming from their direction.

Two Japanese guards had been posted just outside the church walls. The ladies said the guards took turns to sleep so we were unable to help the family in any way. On the fourth morning the door was unlocked by a Jap, who held his nose as he swung the door open. He looked at the mess inside then walked away. As he got to the open doorway of the church he turned around and shouted, 'Feed family, clean room.'

There was hardly any movement within; we were convinced they were all dead. It was one of the nuns who went in first. I remember being ushered out of the way, but I caught a glimpse of the crumpled bodies lying next to each other. The children were sent outside and we all waited by the door of the church. The whole family was helped out into the sunlight and over to the washing area as the nuns bathed the encrusted dirt from their skeletal bodies. Their faces were almost black, except for two lines of white where their almost constant tears had washed the grime away. They were no longer crying; Mama said they were cried out. Their eyes were closed and it took them an age to open them even a little and let in the bright sunshine. As they gradually opened their eyes their faces twisted with pain and they instinctively put up their hands to block out the sun.

The nuns gave them water to drink and allowed them a little fruit, and then they were taken away to the hospital. It took a good ten minutes for them to shuffle the fifty metres across the compound to the door that led into the hospital. They were there for a week before they came back into the main church building. Margaret appeared to have made a good recovery, but the children were never the same again. They didn't join in the games we asked them to play and they never smiled. Young Thomas spent all of his time just lying on his bed in the church, and then one day he disappeared.

One day there was a great commotion in the camp. A number of Japanese military had arrived in army trucks.

'It must be another *tenko*,' I said to Mama, but this time she shook her head. Somehow I realized that this *tenko* was a little different.

The Japanese officer lined us up and for once did not demand our names or cardboard numbers. He explained that all single girls from seventeen years and upwards were to line up separately. Everyone suddenly looked suspicious and the young girls looked very frightened. Some of the girls clung to their mothers, not wanting to join the line that was slowly taking shape.

Eventually there was a long line of about thirty girls, each one trembling with fear. Several Japanese officers appeared, walking up and down the line, looking at the girls very carefully. The officers were laughing among themselves; occasionally they would take hold of the chin of a particular girl, study her and make a comment to one of their colleagues.

The poor girls just stood there, frightened, heads down, not daring to look up. The discussions continued and some of the girls were dismissed. Eventually the line was down to ten.

Some of the mothers were crying and pleading with the Japanese officers to let their daughters go. The girls were ordered to pack a bag and report immediately to the front gate, where a truck was waiting to take them to a different camp. At the gate the mothers had gathered to protest to the officers. The girls were saying their goodbyes and hugging their mothers and friends. As they were forced into the trucks, an officer spoke to one of the mothers.

'Do not worry,' he said, 'girls will be safe. They provide comfort for soldiers of the Imperial Japanese Army.'

CHAPTER 15

'Ik ga nog liever dood'

❦

It was the lack of food that tired me out so quickly. We had been at the camp nearly eight months and I had noticed that I was starting to take to my bed in the afternoons. I would fall asleep for two hours, sometimes three, and awake with hunger pains clawing at the lining of my stomach. I wasn't the only one. Mama and Karin dozed off most days now. I had a fear that we were slowly starving to death and that one day I would go to sleep and not wake up. It was a real relief every time I opened my eyes.

One afternoon I awoke to the scent of something very unpleasant and yet more than familiar. Even though the hygiene in the camps was minimal and the smell of sweaty unclean bodies almost constant, the Japanese guards on the whole were immaculately turned out, with clean white shirts poking over the collars of their uniform.

There was one Japanese guard, however, who stank. His

uniform looked a little dirtier than that of his soldier friends, his hair a little greasier and his teeth were almost green. His officer was always scolding him, but he was just one of a handful who always looked dirty, no matter how much he washed. If he spoke on parade his sour breath could be smelled metres away. We nicknamed him the Nip; he had a tiny screwed-up face like a rat's, which you could just imagine a handful of whiskers protruding from. The smell that came from his body could quite easily be that of a sewer rat rolling around in the filth and waste of the smelliest sewer in Surabaya.

The smell of the Nip had woken me.

My body tensed up immediately. What was he doing in the church at this time of day? He should not be here. A feeling of panic welled up inside me as the smell grew stronger and I became aware of him standing over me. As my eyes opened, I gradually grew accustomed to the light and breathed a sigh of relief as he slowly walked away. I was not the focus of his attention: his eyes were fixed on one of the young Dutch girls who had also been sleeping but was now standing on the floor, stretching and combing her fingers through her hair. She was wearing a thin white blouse, which hung down just above her knees, and the shape of her tiny body underneath was exposed by the light streaming in through the door behind her.

The Nip was grinning and sneering; he had an evil look on his face, the like of which I had never seen before. He took a quick look around the church. It was quiet – there were no more than fifteen or twenty sleeping bodies spread around – and the girl was oblivious to his presence. As he walked towards her I thought she was blocking his route out of the church and I willed her to move out of the way. The Nip took the last few steps towards her and grabbed her roughly by the arm.

The girl instinctively resisted, trying to pull away, but he slapped her across the face and snarled at her to obey him. The girl froze for a moment, clearly shocked. The guard pulled at her arm again and dragged her away from the bunks; he pulled her over to the darkness of the store cupboard area and their voices grew louder. The guard took a key from his pocket and opened the door to one of the store cupboards while hanging onto the girl with the other hand. In one quick movement he had pushed her inside and he stood for a moment in the doorway. Time seemed to stand still. There was no noise from inside the store cupboard and the guard just stood with his hands on his hips. I could not see his evil grin, but I knew it was spread right across his face.

He took a step forward and started fumbling with the front of his trousers. He said a few words:

'Girl will be good.' And then his thick leather belt fell to the floor.

It was like a signal to the girl inside as she flew out of the room in a rage. The guard grabbed her in a bear hug and lifted her body from the floor as he tried to take the few short steps to the opening of the room. She was yelling now and people were beginning to wake up and wonder what was going on, yet no one lifted a finger to help her. The girl had placed her feet on either side of the door frame, and even though the guard pushed with all his might, he could not get her through the gap.

She was shouting at him in her native tongue: 'Ik ga nog liever dood! Ik ga nog liever dood!'

I knew enough of the Dutch language to know that the poor creature was shouting that she'd rather die.

She managed to turn her face towards him and spat at him. He dropped her immediately and she fell heavily onto the floor. He lashed out at her with his boot as he desperately tried to wipe at his wet face. It was only then that I noticed the poor girl was naked; her blouse had been torn from her in the struggle.

The Nip was shouting and screaming at her, but seemed more concerned with the spittle running down his face. The girl lay on the floor groaning, clutching at her stomach. I expected him to continue with the beating, but instead he turned and walked from the church.

The girl was not badly hurt and some of the ladies dressed her and wiped away her tears. She could not control her trembling body and the ladies tried to tell her to calm down, but she just kept looking up at the open door of the church, her eyes tormented with fear. Even I knew the Nip would want revenge. The girl had spat in the face of a Japanese soldier; it was surely one of the worst things she could ever have done. A Japanese delegation of half a dozen soldiers breezed into the church soon after and stood to attention by the door. A minute later the officer in charge of the camp marched in. The girl was sitting on the bunks surrounded by attentive women. He waved them away and the girl looked up at him as she cowered in fear.

'Stand,' he said quietly and the girl did as she was commanded, instinctively bowing as she stood.

He spoke gently; for once he did not shout. 'It is true you spat in face of soldier of Japanese Imperial Army?'

The tears were rolling down her cheeks as she answered. 'He attacked me.'

'Answer question.'

'He attacked me, he was—'

The officer interrupted. 'Answer question.'

The poor girl had nowhere to go; the officer did not want to know what one of his soldiers had done.

The girl nodded.

The officer turned round to face the remaining ladies and children who were in the church. 'All out,' he announced. He raised his voice slightly. '*Tenko* . . . immediately.'

We had been standing on parade for an hour when they dragged the girl out. She could not stand. Her arms and legs were a mass of cuts and bruises and her eyes were puffed up and closed. Her once white blouse was stained red and brown with dirt and looked like a torn old piece of rag. God knows what they had done to her. She was like a rag doll. The soldiers left her to stand, but she flopped onto the ground. As always, the nuns appeared from nowhere as soon as the soldiers walked away. The nuns had her; she would be better now, I thought to myself. This was always the effect the nuns had. They were kind and told nice stories and made people better with their medicines. I looked at the poor girl being lifted onto the stretcher and, even though she looked near to death, I just knew the nuns would patch her up again and she would be back with us soon.

I waited for weeks to see the Dutch girl but she never came back.

CHAPTER 16

Please Buddha, Give Us Some Food

~⋙⋘~

September 1944

The nuns had called a meeting and I convinced myself that it was to tell us the Dutch girl would be coming back. Perhaps it was a surprise? Perhaps they would be bringing the girl with them?

In the meeting one of the nuns, Sister Maria, told us about a list of families.

She explained that the church camp was getting overcrowded and that some families had to be moved on to other facilities. She spoke reassuringly, telling us that the food would last longer with less people in the camp, and that the families who had to leave would get better accommodation and food where they were going. I began to wonder what it would be like to leave this place I had known as my home for so long. I wondered about the old nuns who served the food and how they had been so kind to me, and I thought about the other ladies who had looked after Mama.

I looked into the eyes of the elderly nun as she spoke . . . and . . . yes . . . I would miss the nuns, too. The church camp had been terrible; I'd witnessed beatings and killings and filth and disease and cruelty beyond belief. Mama had become very ill, Karin too, and the food that we had been served for over eight months was simply awful. So why was I looking at the list that Sister Maria held out at arm's length and praying that our name was not included?

She began to read out the names of twelve families who would be leaving first thing in the morning after breakfast:

'Van Beek; Buyse; Smith; Pieters; Willems; Dubois; Grønn-Nielsen . . .'

The remaining names were a blur. She also told us we had to prepare ourselves for a long walk and announced that we would get a little more porridge the following morning and an extra banana. Lasse and Karin were smiling when the kindly old nun mentioned the banana. I looked at Mama. She looked frail, and although the swelling in her legs had gone down a little, I doubted whether she could survive a short walk, let alone a march. She even seemed to struggle getting over to the kitchen area in the garden. This was not good news. I looked at my friends who would be staying behind, and my fellow band members, Jaap and Arnie, and started to say my goodbyes and make our plans for the morning.

In the end the promise of an extra banana did not materialize. At breakfast the following morning we received only one banana between the four of us. Sister Maria apologized and said the Japs had promised extra bananas but that they hadn't arrived. I refused to let Karin and Lasse eat it there and then and put it in my rucksack for later. I felt glad I had pilfered extra bread and rice the evening before. After we left I filled up all of the water bottles and made everybody drink until they could drink no more. Karin complained that her belly was too full. I laughed inwardly: I had not heard her say that in a long time.

The gates were opened and we stepped outside the compound for the first time in nearly nine months. I pushed aside the nice memories of the friends I had made, the makeshift orchestra and the games we had played, and tried to convince myself that we were heading somewhere better. The Japanese commandant stood outside and read out the names of the families as he counted us.

It was now September 1944 and Lasse was nearly two years of age. Many of the other women and children stood at the entrance of the gate and waved us off. There were lots of tears, especially among the children, and for once the Japs made no attempt to close the gates as the families that were left behind watched us disappear from view.

We had been walking just a short while when I started to notice the scenery around us. It was the colours that hit me first. The church camp had no flowers, no grass and only a couple of trees. The ground was grey, the walls were grey, the toilets and hospital block a dirty shade of white. All of a sudden I was looking at colours I had been deprived of for so long. The flowers were in full bloom, beautiful shades of yellow, red, deep pinks and purples, and because of the recent rains the trees and flowers were surrounded by a carpet of green grass and shrubs. It lightened my spirits, even though we did not know where we were heading. Then a few minutes later I heard a beautiful noise we had not heard for so long: birdsong.

I looked in the trees and bushes to seek the tiny creatures out as they tweeted a chorus when we walked by. They had never been seen or heard in the church camp. Why should they have been? Our prison had lacked food, or even a bush for them to perch on. Our prison had been home to a thousand starving wretched souls; no berries, no fruit, no leftovers, like the bread and peanuts we would leave out on our veranda in Surabaya. These birds were free and could fly anywhere they wanted, build their nests in bushes laden with berries or in trees next to the fruit plantations, which had well-irrigated loose soil crawling with succulent worms and beetles for their young. Our prison camp offered them nothing except a fight or two with a rat for a few crumbs of bread.

We passed beautiful fruit orchards and plantations of bananas and mangoes and still the birds sang on. We saw the native butterflies of Java, some as big as my hand, with distinctive yellow and black wings. They seemed almost to follow our desperate march, fluttering above our heads as if pleased with the company along this normally quiet road.

For the first hour or two I enjoyed a pleasant walk in the beautiful Javanese countryside, but then we ran out of water and food and the focus of our attention was on how long we would be walking and where the next drop of water was coming from. Mama had a few centimetres of water in her bottle, which she had been sipping since we set off. She would not let any of us drink from it, explaining that the nuns had managed to give her some painkillers, which she had put in her water. I looked down at her legs as she drank the last few drops. They were all swollen at each ankle and I wondered how on earth she'd walked so far.

'I hope it's not much further, Lisemor,' she said. 'Another hour or two and this medicine will wear off.'

'Don't worry, Mama,' I replied. 'I'm sure it won't be much further now.'

Lasse and the other children were complaining of thirst and tiredness now. Like me, they had enjoyed the first few hours as a kind of freedom, something they hadn't been used to.

The Japanese told us to rest and we sat under a huge banyan tree that shaded us from the sun. There were four guards and they sat a short distance away. They ate pieces of fruit they had picked en route and one of them sliced off the skin of a large pineapple with his machete, which he then shared with his colleagues. I watched as they munched on the sweet flesh and the saliva literally ran down my chin.

Mama was rearranging her cardboard shoes. We had been captive for more than one year and most of the adults' shoes had simply fallen apart. Before the march had started, some of the mothers had tied pieces of cardboard to the bottom of their feet with strips of bandage. It offered a little protection against the sharp stones and biting insects along the way. The children had long outgrown their shoes, so we were all barefoot. We were used to having no shoes, though, and the soles of our feet were like leather. Mama said we were very lucky as her feet were still very tender. She discarded the bandage that by now was in shreds and replaced it with another bandage that she took from her bag.

Just then I remembered the banana we had been given that morning. By now it had almost turned black, but I managed to peel it and divide it into four equal pieces.

Before long the Japanese guards shouted at us to stand and we assembled on the dusty road once again before being ordered to start walking.

My stomach told me it was lunchtime and the sun was at its fiercest, but still the guards made us walk on. The ladies had taken anything they could to shade the children from the sun. Some were lucky enough to have hats but others covered their heads with cloths and leaves. We used some of Lasse's nappies.

By now the birds and butterflies had disappeared into the shade of the bushes and the flies had come out to annoy us. They settled on the beads of sweat at the back of my neck and I swatted at them continuously with the back of Lasse's nappy. Lasse wanted to be carried permanently now, and at first Karin and I took turns, aware that Mama could not physically lift him. The other ladies without young babies also lent a hand and Lasse dozed off in many different arms.

We were walking in an almost permanent cloud of dust, thrown up by feet that no longer walked, just shuffled. We longed for shade and water, but the sun was directly above us and the Japs shouted for us to hurry on. I hated the Japanese, who somehow seemed to have a never-ending supply of water, which they would not share with anyone. I thought back to the handcart that had sat by the church compound gate. How easy it would have been to load a handcart like that with water and get some of the women to push it? Women and children were begging the guards for water, but they just ignored us.

We passed fields full of pineapples and some of the mothers asked the guards if the children could pick them. They refused.

Mama had developed a sway once again, the same sway she'd had on the previous march to the church compound. She was not going to make it, I was convinced of it. I urged her on and told her it couldn't possibly be much further.

We passed fields of plantations, papaya, mango. I remembered back in Surabaya the smell of the ripe fruit, and although our parents forbade us to steal from the trees, it was impossible to resist. We organized ourselves into gangs and planned the raids very carefully. The rewards were always worth the risk and I didn't remember ever being caught. I remembered the taste and juiciness of the fruit; now those memories seemed like a long time ago.

'I'm afraid the painkillers are wearing off, Lisemor,' Mama said.

I looked up the road and could see a few buildings in the distance.

'Hang on, Mama, we are nearly there,' I said. 'Perhaps we are at our destination, or at least they will have water.'

Mama looked up from the road and forced a half-smile.

'Perhaps,' she said. 'Perhaps.'

Everyone's spirits lifted as we approached the village; even Lasse opened his eyes and wanted to walk for a while.

I watched the soldiers like a hawk, looking for some small sign that they were preparing to stop. I was almost on the verge of tears as we walked right through the village without slowing down. I was so, so hungry and thirsty. Some of the children burst into tears when it was clear we weren't stopping, but the Japs kept on going. A few locals stood at the edge of the village and stared. A couple of dogs moved between the people, having a good smell.

The villagers looked on sympathetically and one old lady drank from a bottle of water. I just knew she wanted to take a step forward and give a little to the children. One of the Japanese guards saw her and stepped towards her. He pointed his bayonet at her chest and told her to move away. I believe the old lady had tears in her eyes as she turned and walked towards her house. Karin asked me why the guard had turned her away and I asked myself the same question. There was no need for it. Surely the village had a well? Surely we had time to stop?

The same Japanese guard took great pleasure in taking out his water bottle and enjoying a long drink in view of everybody as we neared the edge of the village. I would have done anything for that bottle of water.

As we walked out towards the open road we came across what can only be described as a shrine, some fifty metres out of the village. As we approached it, the Japs started to take off their packs, and I realized we were about to stop. The broad grins of the children and mothers opened up as we stood directly in front of the most amazing, colourful sight I had ever seen. Underneath the most beautiful tree, adorned with hanging pink flowers, sat a huge fat man made of stone. I had seen the man several times before in Surabaya: it was a statue of Buddha. But this was no ordinary Buddha; this was a very special Buddha, as the ground to the side and in front of him was a beautiful carpet of pink and yellow flower petals. Hundreds of tiny candles had been placed on top of the petals and hung in the branches of a tree. I remember wondering, because there were so many, how they didn't set the branches on fire.

I stood gazing at the colourful shaped pieces of paper fluttering above the stone statue.

'Prayer flags,' Mama said as I looked high into the tree.

But I didn't look into the tree for very long because my focus was now on what surrounded Buddha. The rest of the children had noticed it, too. I counted at least twenty hand-painted identical bowls. In the bowls were pieces of pineapple, bananas, mangoes and rice, lots of rice, and every bowl was polished and shiny and arranged nicely. On a plinth in front of Buddha was a tray of biscuits and glasses of water, some coloured yellow, red and green. It was a feast, I thought to myself, and I looked on as a family of villagers walked up to the statue and placed a bowl of bright-orange boiled sweets on the ground.

I was so excited; the villagers had laid on a feast just for us. I looked at the soldiers and then at Mama, waiting for a signal or command that we could begin to eat and drink. Some of the other children were already edging forward in anticipation, nervously smiling at their mothers and the villagers. Just then a Javanese family came up the road with yet another bowl filled with fruit. A little girl about Karin's age held the bowl. I noticed that she was very thin and how sad she looked. She was saying something to her father and pointing at the fruit. Her father shook his head and took the bowl from her. He walked over to Buddha, bowed his head, said a few words and placed the bowl on the ground. As he walked back over to his daughter, she began to cry.

I looked at Mama. 'Can we eat and drink now, Mama?' I asked. 'Surely they have brought us enough food?'

Mama had slumped to the ground, as had most of the other mothers, glad of the rest and the shade of the durian tree. She massaged the back of her legs as she spoke. 'It is not for you, Lisemor.'

I didn't understand.

'What do you mean, it's not for me? There's water and fruit and biscuits, and the people of the village are bringing it for us. They do not want it and the Japanese soldiers do not seem as if they want it, so who can it be for?'

Mama pointed straight ahead.

'It's for him.'

It did not make sense. Mama was pointing in the direction of the stone statue. There was no one else around or anywhere near him.

'Who, Mama, who is it for? You are pointing at no one.'

'I am pointing at Buddha, Lisemor. I am pointing at the man of stone. Everything is for him.'

I laughed out loud. I thought Mama was playing a joke, but then I realized everyone was so hungry and thirsty that she couldn't possibly be joking. I looked around at the children and the Japs and the villagers, who all just stood and stared. No one made any attempt to take any of the food. Some of the villagers were bowing and humming quietly; the little girl was still sobbing and staring at the pretty bowls of fruit, biscuits and cakes.

'But, Mama, it's a piece of stone, he cannot eat; his mouth is fixed and cannot open.' I looked at the little girl's father, who was now rocking back and forth with his hands cupped together.

'They are offering their God gifts, Lisemor. They are giving their God the finest food from their table as a sign of their faith in him.'

'But they are hungry, too,' I cried out in exasperation. 'Look at the girl, she is thinner than me. She cannot take her eyes from the fruit. Buddha cannot eat.'

'I know, Lisemor,' she said. She pointed down the path. I followed the direction of her finger. 'And there is yesterday's feast and the day before and the day before that.'

Flies and wasps hovered and buzzed over a large cardboard box. I could make out the shape of an almost black banana, a big chunk of pineapple and a green mouldy cake and I wanted to cry as I realized that none of us would be taking part in the feast. We were starving and thirsty and there was food and water in abundance, but not a drop would pass anyone's lips . . . not even Buddha's.

'But this is stupid, Mama.' I looked at the villagers. 'They are stupid and they are blind. Can't they see the rotten food down the path? Don't they realize that the fat stone man cannot eat?'

Mama sighed. 'They see it, Lisemor. They see it fine and they put the food into the rubbish piles every few days and they see their gifts going to the flies and the mice and the rats, not to Buddha.'

'Then why do they still do it, Mama . . . why?'

'They do it because the men of religion tell them they must do it. They do it because of religion.'

Now I was more confused than ever. I thought back to the nuns from the church compound. The nuns were the nicest, kindest ladies I had ever met and Mama said they were religious. I asked Mama about the nuns; they looked after everyone, gave the ill medicine and attended the sick. Surely the nuns' religion was a good religion and this Buddha religion was stupid because they were taking good food from the hungry children and giving it to the rats and mice.

Mama looked up at me and then across at Buddha.

'You are a ten-year-old girl and you are already wise beyond your years. You can see the rotting food and how stupidly the villagers are acting. Look at the Japs, too. Even they dare not take a morsel of food from Buddha's dining table, nor will they let us, either. They are frightened of the stone man.'

Mama wiped a tear from her eye. 'They are stupid.'

'But, Mama, the nuns, they—'

'Forget it, Lisemor,' she interrupted. 'They are all very kind and helpful and yet they sat and watched as girls were beaten and murdered in their so-called house of God. Afterwards they told us it was his will, and they tell us how magnificent he is and how he will look after all of his children.'

Mama's lip was trembling now and she kept looking over at Buddha's feast as she spoke.

'Well, where is he now? And why isn't he looking after his little children? Why does he not allow a single drop of water to pass their lips?'

As Mama mumbled her tirade under her breath, the guards made us stand up and prepare to start walking again. And as we moved out I watched in agony as the fruit, rice, biscuits, sweets and water lay untouched, already beginning to spoil in the heat of the full sun shining on the shrine.

I do not know how we managed to make it to the camp of Lampersarie. I do not know why people did not die, especially Mama. The painkillers had long worn off and she walked for at least one hour in agony, starving and literally dying of thirst. We had probably walked for only a few hours, but it felt like years. The guards began to fuss around us, barking that now we had only a little way to go, and hitting some of the adults with bayonets, so the blood poured.

With great effort, we took it in turns to carry the young, who had fallen asleep. The elderly and sick also needed assistance to move on. Not one of the guards offered to carry any baggage.

They just laughed viciously, shouting that we had to hurry up: 'Wretched creatures!'

It was a long time since we had encountered human beings. Now there were only grey, dry fields as far as we could see. 'This place must be far from Semarang,' the adults whispered among themselves, 'and in the opposite direction to where the monastery is located.' In a haze, we approached a cluster of tall trees and there, once again, was the eternal barbed wire fence. It stretched as far as the eye could see, and beyond it lay a lot of small houses and barracks.

We were chased towards a kind of main building with an impressive portal, which had probably been a great reception at a military compound once. The hated Japanese war flag hung slackly down the flagpole. I also seem to remember that 'Lampersarie' was written over the entrance portal. Everything was decaying and overgrown. Even the barbed wire fence was old and rusty, though still uncomfortable to touch. In some places it had plaited bamboo partitions, closing off all access from the curious natives.

Next we were herded some thirty metres further down to a big side gate, where lorries and essential supplies were being taken through. A dozen Japanese soldiers received us with the usual angry orders, most of which we never really understood. What we now did understand, however, was '*tenko*'.

I tried desperately hard not to fall to the ground as my legs trembled and my knees knocked together. Lasse was crying for water, but Mama and Karin just stood and stared straight ahead.

We watched as the officer in charge marched out in front of us. He nodded at one of his soldiers, who came forward to get some paperwork from the guards who had walked with us. Another soldier came out with glass bottles of water for the four guards, and I could see from the condensation around the glass that they had been stored somewhere very cold. One of the guards took a drink and even poured some over his head to cool himself down. It was simply too much for some of the smaller children, who collapsed into the dirt.

A lady took a step forward and bowed her head in the direction of the officer.

'Please, sir,' she asked politely, 'would it be possible for the children to take some water? Some have not had a drink for several hours.'

The officer clenched his fists and began to shout at the woman in Japanese. Then, without warning, he hit the woman in the face with his fist. As she fell to the floor he stood over her and unclipped his leather pouch, which held his gun. He took it out and pointed it at her head, yelling at her in Japanese. The lady curled up in a ball and covered her head with her hands. I was sure he was about to kill her there and then as he ranted on, getting angrier and angrier. Again I asked myself, why?

The new Japanese guards took at least an hour to read out the names of the fifty people who had made the long trek between the two prison camps. At times my vision blurred as I looked at the face of the guard reading the names; sometimes there were two of him, sometimes even three. Then they read out names, numbers and streets. The Grønn-Nielsen family were staying at number 34 Blimbong Street. I would remember number 34 as it was the year in which I was born. As the Grønn-Nielsen address was read out I thought that at last we would be on our way to the house, where we would be able to get water.

It was not to be.

The wait went on and on. We had to wait while everyone was told where they were staying. It was two hours before we were allowed in through the gates, and still the sun shone down on us. Some of the smaller children edged over to the side of a hut to seek some shade, and thankfully the Japanese soldiers didn't seem to mind. I stood with Mama as she leaned on me and at last we were given the order to move into the camp. We trudged through the huge gates topped with barbed wire and, almost instantly, I noticed the drabness. The flowers and butterflies were gone, and there were no trees or songbirds.

CHAPTER 17

The Third Camp: Lampersarie.
Life on a Blue Door

❧❦❧

We were back in another grey hell, and it seemed more depressing than any camp we had come from. We walked forever, stopping at each street while families were pointed in the direction of their new houses. We walked past a flat concrete platform about the size of a small hockey pitch. There was no shade on the platform and, as we passed, I could feel the rise in temperature. I imagined the concrete baking in the sun as it absorbed the rays. It looked so out of place, like the start of a building structure that had never been completed.

Mama did not now have the energy to answer my questions, so I stopped asking. Finally there were only four of us left. We walked past buildings and more streets. The camp was like a huge village. People were staring at us; they were not friendly. I would later learn that they were already overcrowded and an extra family meant an even bigger squeeze. As we were guided towards one of the houses that looked almost derelict, the only thing that stood out against our grey world was a blue door, which lay upon two concrete posts embedded in the ground. The windows were strange-looking and I couldn't quite put my finger on what was different about the windows we'd had in our house in Surabaya. I would later discover that the occupants of the house had hollowed out a gap from the bottom of each window so that they could be used as makeshift doors.

From the outside the house was a sorry mess, but I convinced myself it would be nicer inside. The Japanese soldier shouted at Mama, 'Your house. Go.'

We were met by a Dutch lady, who tried to explain where we would be sleeping. She introduced herself as Mrs Antje.

Mama said, 'Please can you give us some water?'

Mama slumped down onto the blue door and Mrs Antje ran into the house. Soon afterwards she returned with a big bottle of water and we all took a long drink. The bottle was empty very soon and Mrs Antje ran in again to refill it.

Mrs Antje once again started to try and tell us where we would be staying, but we were only interested in drinking till our bellies ached. Lasse and Karin were severely dehydrated and Mama looked simply awful.

After a few minutes Mrs Antje eased Mama to her feet.

'We'll get you some food as soon as we have sorted out the sleeping arrangements.'

She explained that we were to be given a choice of where to sleep; it would be a tight squeeze whatever we chose, Mrs Antje said as she showed us around the crowded house. I felt like lying down. I just wanted to sleep, and I was hungrier than I could remember ever having been, but I was curious and fought the urge. I also had a strange feeling that we might have to fight for a decent place to stay. The other ladies and children in the house eyed us with suspicion and distrust. Mrs Antje told us that she was living in a hallway with three other Dutch teachers and there was simply no room for a family of four.

'I assume you want to sleep together,' she said.

Mama nodded her head wearily.

Our choice was straightforward: a storeroom or the main lounge with fifteen people. Mama looked around the hostile faces in the lounge and said to Mrs Antje, 'Please, how can we squeeze any more in here?'

Mama was upset and almost crying. We had walked forever in the hope that we were going somewhere better, to a camp with more room, more food and kinder guards, and now the awful realization had set in. I could see the desperation in poor Mama's eyes and that she almost seemed to be giving up. Mrs Antje walked us through to the storeroom and I noticed that the occupants of the lounge started to smile. One or two of them even followed us through to the corridor and offered to help us clean the store cupboard up.

I had never seen anything quite like the room we were shown. The walls were covered in a bluey-brown fungus and huge dusty cobwebs draped from every corner. I don't think anyone had been in that room for many years. How on earth were we expected to sleep in that filthy, tiny place? I thought there wasn't enough room for two bodies to lie down, never mind four.

The smell hit me as soon as the door was opened and Mama recoiled as it hit her too. Poor Lasse burst out crying as he looked in and Karin almost collapsed. One of the ladies led Karin, Lasse and me outside, and my brother and sister flopped down onto the blue door. They both lay down under the shade of a sorry-looking tree. I looked at its branches and the few leaves that adorned it and thought to myself, even the trees are hungry and thirsty here.

I so wanted to join them – my body cried out for rest – but I thought about Mama and that awful room and knew I needed to look in on what was being done.

I stepped back through the opening to the house.

One of the women from the lounge was holding pieces of cardboard and another had appeared with a brush.

'We can't sleep in there,' I sniffed between the tears.

Mama put a hand around my shoulders to reassure me. 'It will be fine, Lisemor, once we have cleaned it up.'

I looked at Mama and thought she couldn't possibly have any energy left to help clean up the disgusting store cupboard. Mrs Antje took some more water out to Lasse and Karin, then she returned and spoke to me. 'We'll get you something to eat in a little while.'

The women tried their best to clean our room. I could not fault them for their effort and I joined in, too. Soon a pile of dirty rubbish lay outside in the back garden area. There were bits of wood, small wheels, old shoes, rags, tin cans and bottles. We had all worked very hard, but when I walked back through to the room it smelled just as bad. The floor was bare now, but I saw that a muddy oily substance covered the floor, an inch thick in some parts. I looked at Mrs Antje in desperation and she called to the ladies, 'Fetch some water. This room needs to be clean for the children.'

Again the ladies put all their effort into the task in hand. I wanted to believe they were being neighbourly and kind, but I suspected their efforts were for themselves, so that they could sleep more easily that night, without another four bodies eating into their precious space.

They scrubbed and washed the room for an hour, screaming as on more than one occasion a mouse or rat ran out from a hole in the wall or crack in the floor. One tap stood upright just along the corridor and Mrs Els, Mrs Antje's teacher friend, stood guard over it the whole time. She told me that the water was precious. Mrs Antje allowed the ladies buckets of water, but made sure there were always containers around the house that were continually full. She explained that the water went off two or three times every week.

Even so, bucket upon bucket of water was poured out onto the concrete floor, then swept outside. The door to the house and our room was open and a warm breeze dried it up a little. I lost count of the number of cockroaches scuttling around the confined space. The ladies would scoop them up on the bristles of a broom and throw them outside.

'Why don't you kill them?' I asked one of the ladies.

She looked at me and frowned.

'Have you ever tried to kill a cockroach?' she asked.

I shook my head.

'It is impossible to kill a cockroach. Even if you cut its head off it will live.'

'It will?'

'Yes, it will live for many days and even then it will only die because it has no mouth and cannot eat so it starves to death.' She rubbed at my hair. 'A bit like us, little one. We are all starving, too.'

As she looked down into the room another cockroach ran across the floor and she stunned it with the head of the broom. It lay on its back, but still its horrible little legs moved and its huge black head twitched from side to side.

The thought of sleeping with these horrible creatures was more than I could take. 'Please make sure you get them all out,' I begged.

'I will try,' she replied.

Mama stood in the doorway, too. 'We cannot put a child on that floor,' she said to Mrs Antje. 'It's disgusting.'

Mrs Antje spoke to her and told her that we all had to make the most of it. But she went through to the lounge area again and, after much argument, returned with a blanket and a dirty-looking rug.

'We will make a bed for the little boy and get him raised up off the ground.'

The women worked hard on the room until it was nearly dark and then we were given some food before bedtime: a bowl of rice and some tasteless, watery soup.

A dirty old mattress and more pieces of cardboard were dragged into the room and Mrs Antje helped Mama build a little bed for Lasse using our rucksacks, the blanket and rug. At least he was off the floor. Our remaining possessions were placed on top of the lone chest of drawers. As darkness fell and we settled down for the night, all I could think of was the cockroach on its back and its horrible black wriggly legs.

Karin and I could not stretch out fully because the room was so small. We lay with our knees tucked into our chests and I was given the responsibility of guarding the door. Mama explained that, as there were no windows in the room, the door would need to stay open all through the night. We tore up some pieces of card and built a sort of barrier at the bottom so the rats, mice and cockroaches could not climb in.

It was, without a doubt, the worst night I have ever spent in my entire life. I was terrified and we were bitten every minute of the night. I hardly slept a wink, all the time clawing at the invisible creatures sinking their teeth into my skin and feeling sure the horrible cockroach with the wriggly legs would try to reclaim his former home during the hours of darkness.

The next morning I cleaned the room some more and took the rug that the ladies had given us out into the sunlight. Mama was sitting with Karin and Lasse on the blue door; they all looked exhausted.

'Come and rest, Lisemor,' Mama called out. 'No one slept last night. Rest a little before we take our breakfast.'

I would not rest until I had rid the rug of those horrible creatures.

'The rug will need cleaning,' I replied. I laid it on the ground and started to beat the dust from it, but I soon realized why the ladies had given up. As I hit it with the old broom, the dust rose into the sunlight and it seemed to be alive with a million creatures that flew into the air. Mama watched, expressionless. I told her not to worry and that if we left it in the sun long enough the heat would do the rest. I beat the rug until I could beat it no more. I did the same with the blanket and left it in the sun for hours before lifting them both back into the room again. I hoped the heat of the sun would have killed anything still living in the rug and blanket.

I went back into the house to ask about breakfast. Mrs Antje confirmed that the Grønn-Nielsens were on a special list for food and said she would take us up to the kitchen area for our rations. I explained that Mama could not make it after such a long walk and asked if I could collect hers and my brother's, too. Karin's curiosity overtook her tiredness and she raised herself to her feet to make the long walk to the breakfast queue. Lasse seemed comfortable with Mama on the blue door and, as Mrs Antje looked outside, she agreed to my request.

'I will agree this time, but your mama and your brother must make an effort in future, otherwise they will get nothing.'

Mrs Antje was very kind; I liked her. She told me that we

would be getting our food for the whole day and we must take care to save a little for lunchtime and supper.

'It's no good eating it all now, Lise, as you will go to bed hungry.'

'Mrs Antje,' I said, 'I have gone to bed hungry for as long as I can remember.'

Mrs Antje laughed, pulled me into her and cuddled me. 'I suppose you have, little one, I suppose you have.'

Mrs Antje gave me what she called four billycans. There was a round billycan for each of us made of tin and they stacked neatly on top of one another. When we got to the kitchen area after a five-minute walk, we stood in a queue for a while. Mrs Antje spoke with one of the women about how the two small girls needed four rations. She told the ladies serving the food that Mama had beriberi and that Lasse was allowed a baby ration. Although the woman did not look happy, she reluctantly served Karin and me with double rations. Porridge was slopped into two cans and rice into the others. The porridge ration for Lasse was topped up with a cup of milk and he also got a banana. As we walked away from the lady serving the rice, a large piece of bread was placed on top of my billycans. Mrs Antje told me it would need to be divided into four.

Mrs Antje took two of the billycans from Karin as they were very heavy and she was struggling to cope with them. It was only about three hundred metres to the blue door, where Mama and Lasse were sitting, but it seemed to take forever to get back.

We sat on the door and ate breakfast and I was careful to tell

Mama what Mrs Antje had said. I persuaded her and Karin to save the rice ration and bread for later in the day.

Mama was worried about the rice and where we could put it so the mice and cockroaches wouldn't get it. I went exploring and found some wire, then I made two handles for the larger billy-can, into which we put all of the rice. Mrs Antje managed to get a hammer and a nail and we hung the billycan on the nail Mrs Antje had banged into the wall. As I looked around I still wasn't happy sleeping in that horrible room. I walked back outside and looked at Mama, Karin and Lasse sitting on the blue door.

It looked similar in size to the floor area of our store cupboard, and I so wanted to carry the door into the room. It would at least mean we were off that filthy, cold concrete floor.

'Tell me what you are thinking, Lisemor,' Mama asked. 'You have that look in your eyes again.'

I explained my idea.

'It looks very heavy, Lisemor, and I'm not so sure it will fit in there.'

'We must try, Mama.'

Mama sighed but, with an enormous effort, she raised herself from the door. We found some more string and Mama used it as a measure. We stretched it out from one corner of the room to another, with Mama holding the string between her forefinger and thumb. We did the same on the other wall and Mama held the string in a different place with her other hand. As we walked outside I began to get excited. Mama measured the door and proudly announced that it would fit. I almost started jumping up and down. Mrs Antje appeared at this point and asked us what we were doing. I couldn't wait to tell her about my fantastic idea.

Mrs Antje smiled, but then she became serious. 'You are forgetting about one thing, little one.'

'What?'

'Even if the door does fit the floor area of your room, it is much too big to get through this doorway.'

As we all walked back through to view the size of the door, I knew that Mrs Antje was right. We stood and looked at the opening. It was tiny in comparison to the blue door Lasse was now sleeping on. How could I have been so stupid?

Mama ruffled my hair. 'Never mind, Lisemor,' she said. 'At least we won't have to lift that big heavy door. I confess I do not know where I would have found the strength to do that.'

I would have found the strength. If necessary I would have lifted it myself. I was devastated. In the short time we'd been there I had grown fond of our blue door. It felt like it belonged to us and I took a strange comfort and warmth from it every time I sat there with my family. It wasn't the most comfortable mattress in the world, but if we could have got it through the doorway and us off the damp concrete, the nights would have been much more bearable. As I looked into Mama's eyes I knew that she felt exactly the same.

CHAPTER 18

The Disappeared

❦

I lay on the door for some hours, unable to raise myself to do anything. However, as I lay there, I felt like I was drawing strength from somewhere and, as I absorbed the rays of the sun, partly shaded by the branches of the tree, I suddenly found the urge to explore. What better place to start than with our new house? I also thought it was time to meet some of our new neighbours.

Inside the house women and children were sleeping everywhere. It was just like the church camp, except that here they were all lying on the cold concrete tiled floors. As I walked into the corridor where Mrs Antje and her friends slept, I realized that it was not a room at all, but an open terrace covered with a roof and that it led onto an open garden area with no grass and no flowers; it was a bare, grey garden, a dustbowl.

At the far end of the garden were two toilets facing each other; the one on the right was marked WC. Several women stood outside the toilet on the right-hand side, forming an orderly queue. I felt the need to go to the toilet, so I walked over to the one on the left-hand side. The door wasn't so much a door as a simple bamboo partition wall leaning against the opening. I lifted it and moved it to one side, and then the smell hit me. There was no toilet, just a hole in the ground and a space for two feet on either side. Flies were buzzing all around my head and it took a huge effort to keep the breakfast in my stomach. I reeled away coughing and spluttering, covering my face with my hand. Some of the women by the other toilet were laughing. I walked over to see what they were laughing at and why they were all queuing in one place.

A lady spoke in Dutch. 'That is the toilet for the desperate ones,' she announced. 'It used to be the toilet for the servants of the house. Our Dutch brothers and sisters supposed it was good enough for the native Indonesians.'

The door opened to the other toilet as a small boy walked out, and I could see that inside it had a ceramic bowl but no seat; the wooden seat had been used for firewood long ago.

A row of old bottles stood against the wall, containing water to clean oneself with. Each family had their own.

The lady spoke again. 'And this toilet,' she pointed, 'was for the chosen ones: the Dutch masters.'

She wiped a piece of cloth across her brow. 'Alas, I fear we are all equal now. Equal, but most certainly inferior to our Japanese rulers.' She smiled. It was a strange smile. A smile of resignation, not happiness.

'Make sure you are never desperate enough to use that toilet, young lady.' She pointed across the garden. 'Time it well and pray to the good Lord above that you do not get dysentery.'

Suddenly the urge to go to the toilet was not that great and I walked back towards the house. I turned right and went through another covered terrace. I peeped into a couple of bedrooms. Bodies were sprawled across the floor, which was divided for privacy by strategically placed bags and suitcases. I started counting the bodies as I walked. It was the groaning that drew me to the next room. I was standing in the lounge area we had briefly looked into the night before. It was daylight and I was puzzled as to why so many people were still sleeping and lying around. I noticed Mrs Antje wiping at the brow of a young girl and I crossed over to her.

'Why are they sleeping?' I asked. 'Why are they lying around?'

The room was crowded with bodies; moaning, groaning bodies; still bodies; bodies that twitched; bodies that slept, and bodies that stared into nothing. I had long since run out of fingers to count on, but I made a mental note in my head.

'They are ill, Lise,' Mrs Antje said. 'They are ill and weak and they have neither the energy nor the inclination to go outside. Some will die, some will live, but life goes on.' She continued to wipe the sweat from the girl's brow. 'This poor mite has malaria. Her mother has yellow fever and her brother beriberi. Others have tuberculosis and dysentery.' Mrs Antje wiped a tear from her eye with the same piece of cloth she had been using on the little girl and I thought to myself that it wasn't such a good idea.

'She has a fever, Lise. She shivers and vomits and sweats for hours every day. There can be little water left in her starving little body. And when we arrived at this camp the bloody Nips told us there were no mosquitoes.' She turned to face me. 'The mosquitoes bite in the middle of the night . . . they bring us the disease.'

'Will I die, Mrs Antje? I don't understand.'

'You won't,' she said. 'How old are you, Lise?'

'Ten.'

She sighed and stood up. She took me by the hand and walked with me outside. 'It is not for the mind of a ten-year-old girl what is going on here. It's as if we hear of a new disease every day.'

I did not understand. Many people lay in bed and then one day they simply vanished. Later, Mama's doctor friend told her there were about eight thousand people in the Lampersarie camp and at any one time more than half of them were lying in their beds with one disease or other. There was little or no medicine for them, and whenever the supplies did come into the camp, they went to the Japs, not to the suffering people.

Mrs Antje was crying now. I sat with her for a little while before she went back inside the house. I walked back through the corridor and out to the blue door. Mama was sitting in the middle, telling Lasse and Karin stories. I squeezed onto the edge and Karin moved along to give me room. Mama tried to smile and started a new story.

'Did I tell you the story back in Surabaya when I nearly lost your sister here?' Mama looked at me and I knew the story that she was about to tell. She had told it a hundred times, but we never, ever grew tired of hearing it.

'Lise was only a tiny baby and the doctor told me it was time to give her solid food as well as milk. I was so pleased as it meant my little baby was growing. You have to remember that your sister was my first child.'

Lasse looked on, sucking at his two middle fingers, and Karin snuggled into Mama's lap, looking up in anticipation, occasionally glancing at the subject of the story as I looked on in silence.

'The doctor suggested we start her off on porridge mixed with a little milk and sugar. "What could be simpler?" he said. "She will enjoy it." Well, she did enjoy it; she couldn't get enough of it, the greedy little thing.'

Lasse laughed and pointed at me.

'But I have to tell you that the porridge did not seem to agree with her and came straight out the other end only a few hours later. I spoke to the doctor and he told me not to worry. I must persevere and Lise's stomach would get used to it.'

Mama was enjoying her captive audience and dragged out the tale as long as she could.

'Lise was losing weight and your father and I were very worried. Still the doctor told us to give her the porridge and still she would eat as much as she could, but now she was being sick, too. It was coming out of both ends and we simply could not stop it.'

Lasse and Karin were laughing together, looking at me occasionally and then back to the storyteller.

'I took her back to the doctor for an examination and I could see that he was worried, too. "I don't understand it," he said. "She is perfectly healthy and she should be able to take solid foods by now."'

Mama explained how the doctor asked her to tell him exactly what she was putting in the porridge.

'I told him: "I mix the porridge flakes with sugar and milk and even put a few drops of cod liver oil in."

"Excellent," the doctor said, "that is perfect. I cannot understand why she cannot digest it."'

Mama looked up; she was building up to the funny bit.

'"So tell me," said the doctor, "how long do you cook the porridge for?"

"Cook the porridge?" I asked. "What do you mean?"

"How long do you boil the porridge for?" asked the doctor.

"Boil the porridge?"

'The doctor gave a huge sigh of relief and then laughed. "You haven't been cooking the porridge?" he said with a look of amazement.

"Cook it? I didn't know you had to cook it."'

By this time we were all laughing. Mama told us how ashamed and embarrassed she had been and how she'd nearly poisoned her firstborn with raw porridge flakes.

It was a story we made her repeat again and again. Mama never had any books in the camp at Lampersarie, but that did not stop her telling us stories. Stories were a lifeline, a tiny grip on a past life, something to hang onto and store in our minds.

Mama told stories of trolls and of her times in Bergen as a child; she told us about the mountains and the rain and the snow and of our trip back to Norway on the ship called *Gneisenau* to see Grandad and Grandma before the war started.

She told us of the fantastic sight in Norway when Mr Winter put his great big blanket of snow over the mountains, covering every nook and cranny in white. When it had stopped snowing, and the weather cleared, the blue sky and the brightness of the snow made for an amazing picture.

The next day people in Bergen would get busy, collect their skis and take the cable car up into the mountains. The weather could change overnight on the west coast of Norway, so you had to make the most of it. Mama loved skiing and took to the slopes with her friends as often as possible. She promised to teach us to ski when we returned to Bergen.

'But it will be freezing, Mama,' I protested.

'Well, yes,' she agreed, 'but we have all sorts of warm clothes, mittens, scarves and hats for this purpose. You will get used to it.'

We much preferred the story where we travelled with Grandad into the mountains to go troll hunting. He told us that trolls live in great big crevasses, well hidden among trees and rocks, or under bridges near roaring waterfalls. Most trolls are ugly and quite scary, whereas baby trolls could be cute, with their funny faces and long, hairy tails.

Grandma had packed a picnic hamper, which we left behind in the car as we started our journey into the beautiful landscape that only Bergen can boast of. Greater Bergen lies cradled in between seven mountains and is the most beautiful city in Norway.

'That must be when it's not raining, then,' I said, 'because it is almost always raining in Bergen.' Mama smiled and had to agree. She continued her story as we cuddled closer together on the blue door in anticipation.

'Finally we walked into some thick undergrowth and the hunting could begin. I held Karin's hand as Lisemor quickly grabbed Grandad's. It was all so scary and exciting as we went closer to the huge rocks and started to explore the caves.

'"This could be just the right place for the trolls to settle," Grandad whispered, and that was when Karin got scared and started to cry. I remember that you, Lisemor, got very annoyed and said, "Now look what you have done, there is no way they will come out now with all this noise!"

'Then granddad came up with very important information: "Trolls really only venture outside during the night, as the sun is very dangerous for them. Just one ray of sunshine is enough to turn them into stone." Karin then calmed down and looked up into the sky, hoping for lots of sun to save us.

'When it was time for lunch we walked back to the car and the hamper packed with all sorts of goodies, which we can only dream about as we are sitting here.'

Mama looked sad and promised to tell us more soon, as Karin and Lasse were fast asleep. This was a blessing, as it gave them some respite from the constant hunger pangs.

It was such a pleasure when Mama could be with us and felt

well enough to tell her stories. Later in the evening, when it was cooler and the stars shone from this huge, incredible blue-black sky, we settled close together on the door, covered in our bed rags to prevent the mosquitoes from attacking. When the moon was up and the crickets made their usual noise, it was like we were at home in Scandinavia Street again.

Of course, every day we asked about Papa. I don't recall Mama ever really going into detail about Papa in Camp Lampersarie, even though we asked and asked. She would always shrug her shoulders and say she didn't know.

CHAPTER 19

Freedom is a Pink and White Dress

❧✦❧

We sat for many hours on the blue door and protected it with our lives. We made a pact that someone would always sit on it to stop another family taking it. We felt it was ours; it was nearest to our bedroom, and if we had to put up with those awful conditions, then we were entitled to it. We ate our meals on the blue door, too, and when the heat of the sun was at its strongest, the shade of the sorry-looking tree made it just about bearable.

Mama also sewed on the blue door. She repaired our clothes and, as Lasse grew out of his nappies, she used the soft white cotton to make shorts for us. Whenever she made up a pair of shorts for me, she always made sure they had two large pockets at the side. Mama knew what I was getting up to in the cook-house area, but by now she didn't care. There were no lessons on morals in the camps; everyone was in the same boat and it was a case of stealing to survive. Looking back, I've no doubt that the

Above left: Lise's father, Daniel Grønn-Nielsen, as a baby (middle) with his two brothers, parents (left and middle), and nursemaid (right); *Above right:* Daniel Grønn-Nielsen in Bergen, Norway, 1932; *Below*: Lise's parents, Kirsten and Daniel, on their wedding day in Java, 1933

Top left: Daniel Grønn-Nielsen in their home in Java, 1933; *Top right*: Mr Verhoog and his wife Maatje, known to Lise as Opa and Oma

Far left: Lise aged 2, 1936
Left: Lise, aged 2, in the family home in Java, 1936

The family's Javanese gardener, baboe (nursemaid) cook and driver

Kirsten Grønn-Nielsen's
passport

Lise and Karin with
their parents, Daniel and
Kirsten, in Java, 1938

Top: Lise, aged 5, riding a horse in Java, 1939; *Above left*: Lise and Karin at home in Java, 1939; *Above right*: Karin and Lise, aged 3 and 5, wearing traditional Norwegian clothes, on a visit to Bergen, 1938

OPPOSITE PAGE: *Top*: Lise and Karin with Mr and Mrs Verhoog, Opa and Oma; *Bottom*: Swimming with their Australian soldier friends in Rangoon, on the journey home after the war, 1945. Front row, left to right: Lise's friend Kitty, Lise, Kitty's sister Marie (who had been a nurse in the camp hospital) and Karin

Right: Lise, aged 13, going skiing with her friends for the first time, 1947

Lise (fourth from the left), aged 13, practising first aid with the Girl Guides, 1947

Lise, aged 14, and Karin, aged 12, enjoying an ice cream in Bergen, 1948

Above: Lise, aged 15, with her father Daniel in Germany, 1949

Below left: Lise in 1953; *Below right*: Lise, aged 20, as a dancing school teacher in 1954

little extras I managed to pilfer helped my whole family make it through to the end of the war.

By now our clothes were almost falling apart and, of course, we were growing out of them. Mama's blouses were also in shreds and she took to wearing just a bra and a pair of shorts most days. I thought that was very naughty. What would Papa have said if he could have seen her walking around like that? I remember finding a beautiful cotton dress one day while rummaging through her bag. It was pink and white with pretty coloured flowers embroidered into it and shiny red buttons all the way down the front. I took it out to Mama, who was sitting on the blue door, and asked her to wear it instead of the rags she was dressed in.

'I will not, Lisemor,' she said. 'That dress is for when the war is over. I need to look decent on the day we walk out of here.'

I understood.

Mama needed to look good on the day we were freed. She also told us about her pure silk underskirt, yellow like a beautiful golden lemon. It was in her bag, too, kept alongside the pretty dress. Occasionally she would take the garment out and allow us to touch it; it felt like the softest thing in the world.

We had lots of pieces of nappies now as Lasse no longer needed them. They were very valuable as any sort of cloth or material was in short supply. Occasionally they were exchanged for fruit and eggs with the native Indonesians on the other side of the fence. I had realized in our last camp that the Indonesians did not like us, but here in Lampersarie they seemed to like us even less. The boys on the other side of the fence were wicked at times and sometimes set up ambushes for us. We would be standing close to the fence, waiting to trade with them, when all of a sudden the boys would jump out from behind a tree or mound of earth and a shower of rocks would rain down on us. The Japs always thought that it was funny when this happened but, on the odd occasion that one of our boys threw a rock back over the fence, the Japs would scold them and sometimes even hit them. One of the Indonesian boys on the other side said that we were now the lower-class citizens and that both the Japanese and the Indonesians hated the Europeans.

However, if we wanted fruit and eggs, we had no option but to wait and talk and barter with these boys and, of course, I realized they wanted the pieces of rag and cloth as much as we wanted a fresh egg. The boys had nothing by way of clothes: most of the time they ran around in little more than a loin cloth, and they were always barefoot. I talked with one boy, who said that since the war had started the shops that sold children's clothes and the material to make them had all closed down. He explained that the pieces of nappy were important to his family as his mama had given birth to twin girls only three weeks ago and they didn't have one nappy between them. I felt so sorry for the boy on the other side of the fence; he looked so sad as he sat cross-legged in the dirt.

'I could get you two nappies,' I said.

His face lit up. 'You could?'

'Yes, my brother no longer needs them. He is two years old now.'

The boy jumped to his feet. 'Oh please, my mama will be so happy.'

Within three or four minutes we had struck a deal. He would get me three eggs for one nappy and three eggs and three bananas for two. I ran back to the blue door and told Mama all about the wonderful piece of trading I'd arranged. Mama cut the nappies with a pair of scissors, explaining that tiny babies didn't need so much material. The strips she'd cut off could be used for repairs, she explained.

The Indonesian boy was not there when I got back, but I did not worry because I knew it would take him a little longer to collect his side of the bargain. I waited and waited and had almost given up when I heard a shout. He was waving the three bananas above his head and in his other hand he carried a small pouch, which I assumed held the eggs.

'I have them,' he shouted. 'I have them.'

I scolded him and told him not to make so much noise, as it would draw the Japs' attention to us.

'Can I see the nappies?' he asked and I held the two pieces of material out towards the fence.

'Do they feel soft?' he went on as he reached through the fence. I held them a little closer. He stroked at the material and sighed.

'Mama will be so happy,' he said as he looked up and smiled.

'You have the eggs, too?' I asked.

He held up the small pouch. 'Yes, I have the eggs,' he said. 'They are for my supper tonight.'

His reply did not make any sense to me; we had agreed a trade and the eggs were—

Without warning he yanked hard on the nappies. I realized almost immediately what his intention was but, before I could pull the nappies away, they had been pulled onto the wrong side of the fence.

'My bananas . . .' I stuttered, 'my eggs, give them to me.'

The boy was doing a jig a yard away from the fence. 'My bananas,' he said, 'my eggs . . . and my nappies.'

'We had a deal,' I begged. 'We agreed on—'

'I do not deal with Europeans,' he sneered. 'I take from them what I want. I have just proved how stupid you all are.'

'But . . . but . . .' I was on the point of tears. I knew I had been tricked and I knew there would be no eggs and no extra bananas. Why had he tricked me? He would never get anything through the fence again. Still he teased me, waving the nappies and the bananas. I put my hand through the fence and tried to grab at the nappies, but he kept them out of reach. By now I was crying, but still he laughed in my face. I was terrified to think what Mama would say and I felt stupid for trusting a boy I had only met that day. After he tired of his fun he slowly walked away and I slumped to the ground.

'Please,' I called after him, 'please, we had a deal.'

I called out until he could no longer hear me.

It took a long time before I summoned up the courage to go back to the house. I had let Mama down; she was sure to scold me for being so stupid and I was terrified at what her reaction would be.

They were sitting in exactly the same position as when I left them. Only now there were no smiles, no anticipation of eggs for supper and bananas for everyone in the morning. For supper there would be nothing and for breakfast the same foul-tasting porridge and a banana for Lasse, if the Japanese suppliers were in a good mood. I was crying as I approached the door and Mama said, 'What is it, Lisemor? Tell Mama what is wrong.'

Mama was worried about me as I'd been away so long, but she could also see that I carried nothing in my hands or my pockets and that the nappies had gone. Mama guessed what had happened before I even told her. She did not shout or scold me. She simply told me not to be so trusting the next time. I had worried for nothing, but as I lay in my dirty bed that evening on the cold damp floor, hungry as usual, I shed a few silent tears, feeling sorry for myself and wondering why the world was such an unfair and unpleasant place.

CHAPTER 20

The Sweet Taste of Dead Flesh
and Penicillin

❧❧❧

Every day in Camp Lampersarie the fit people were put to work, sweeping roads, cleaning toilets and unblocking drains. Workers for the various kitchen areas were always needed. Poor Mama was never fit enough, but it was probably just as well. Some mornings I was woken by the shouts of the Japanese calling the poor individuals to work. They shuffled out to the kitchen area at six thirty in the morning, hoping for an extra crust of bread or a little porridge, but they were always disappointed. There they were designated their work detail for the day, and sometimes they did not return until after dark.

Studying the poor souls, I do not know how they worked at all. They looked close to death. There were about eight ladies from our house who were in the working parties. I watched as they took the rice and bread they had saved and then ate as if they had never eaten in their lives. They spoke little; the smiles had been taken from them and they drank water from bottles before collapsing into their designated sleeping areas each evening. At six thirty the following morning it started all over again. Occasionally a few of the ladies would be excused because of illness or exhaustion, and sometimes new ladies would replace them; quite often some would join the ranks of the disappeared.

The older children, including myself, would be assigned to collect the rubbish from around the camp and take it to the bins. At first I thought this might be a good opportunity to find discarded food, as I mopped up the rubbish bags from the kitchens – an odd banana skin perhaps or a piece of stale bread. I searched those bins and rubbish heaps for days but found nothing. In the end I gave up. It was as if every scrap or morsel of food, every grain of rice and crumb of bread, had miraculously vanished into thin air.

Food was unbelievably precious and there are many moments that stick in my memory. I recall being incredibly jealous of Lasse. Sometimes, as he ate his banana or his milky porridge, Karin and I would sit watching him after our breakfast had long disappeared and we'd fight to see who could scrape the banana skin or lick out his bowl to taste a precious drop of milk. I always thought Mama could give us at least a little bit of his banana, but she never did, explaining that because he was under three he needed the extra proteins, calcium and vitamins to help him grow. She told Karin and me on more than one occasion that we had had everything we needed in our first few years and Lasse would get as much as she could give him. We understood – sort of – but it never stopped the arguments.

Until you have experienced the pain of hunger, and I mean pain, not just a rumbling in the belly or a little cramp, you cannot possibly understand how bad the conditions were and how we craved and thought about food every minute of the day. We were continually on the lookout for anything we might be able to eat. For me, every time I went to the kitchen area was an opportunity to pilfer a little extra or to look for a grain of rice on a table top that I might be able to slip into my mouth without anyone noticing.

I felt for Mama, too, as she tried to push her rations on to us to fill our bellies, but I also remembered what the older ladies had said in the church camp and made Mama eat her fill as well. Even the food we did get was of very poor quality. The bread was always a few days old, sometimes even older, and it was not unusual to turn the bread over and find green mouldy fungus growing along one side. I remember finding an old loaf in the breadbin in Surabaya in this condition and Mama taking it outside, holding her nose and telling me that it was going in the bin.

Not here.

Everything was eaten, no matter what condition it was in. Mama told us that mould was penicillin and that it was good for us. She persuaded us that the bread was not bad and if we dipped it into our soup it would taste just fine. I held my nose and bit into the penicillin-contaminated bread. I chewed it for several seconds and swallowed. Mama was right: it didn't taste so bad after all. The bread was always hard and stale, so most days we needed to dip it into soup or water just to soften it enough so it wouldn't break our teeth. We had to be careful . . . our teeth were not in good condition either; it was at least a year since our toothbrushes had fallen apart.

Mama was suffering from beriberi, malaria and arthritis, and she spent most of the week in hospital. I visited her every day and made sure that Karin and Lasse always got their rations, and sometimes a little bit more. Karin had given up the walk to the kitchen area now, she was simply too weak, and although I complained and tried to encourage her, I could see that her legs were incredibly thin and realized the enormous effort it took for her to walk just a few steps. As for Lasse, he just slept. And when he did wake up I noticed his smile had also gone, just like the ladies in the house. No one smiled, no one laughed, we just survived.

There was one place in the camp where the battle for survival was at its strongest and that was in the queue for food. The tension at times was unbearable and everyone watched each other like a hawk. Fights would break out for little or no reason: someone thought to be jumping the queue or getting a few more grains of rice than the last person. I didn't mind the fights and learned to use them to my advantage. A fight meant a distraction and a distraction meant a chance to steal or eat the rations you had been given in an attempt to fool the server that she hadn't dished out your ration after all.

No one was immune from accusations. An English lady in the queue one morning accused the Dutch lady serving the rice of favouring her Dutch friends with larger helpings. Two Dutch ladies in the queue behind the English woman started to argue with her and told her not to be so silly. I recall looking in both billycans and I could not tell the difference. The English lady would not be calmed down and, as their voices grew louder, she slapped one of the Dutch women across the face. That was the signal for a full-blown fight, with punches thrown, hair pulled and faces clawed. It was also the cue for Lise Grønn-Nielsen to help herself to three extra bananas. As people looked on and tried to break up the fight, I managed to stuff the bananas deep into my purpose-made pockets, take the rations I was due and quietly slip away while the fight continued.

The Japs never broke up the fights; they would simply look on, smiling. It gave a little entertainment to their otherwise monotonous days. After the fights were over, two or three Japanese guards sometimes dragged one of the women away to one of their offices or huts for punishment.

Even when I returned with the extra bananas it was not enough to cheer Mama up. She was now very depressed and, when she wasn't in hospital, she would simply drag her blanket out and sit on the blue door, staring into space or just crying. She would wake in the middle of the night, crying and complaining of cramp in her legs. She had developed mouth ulcers and sores on her arms and legs, and one day a doctor friend came to our house with fresh tomatoes, which she made Mama eat in front of her.

The doctor explained that the tomatoes would make her better. She gave a tomato to Karin, too, as she had started to develop sores on her elbows and knees.

One day I caught Karin picking at the scabs on her legs and eating them.

'What are you doing?' I asked. She told me they tasted nice, quite sweet. It had been many months since we had tasted sugar from the fly hunts and I watched with envy as she chewed on her dead flesh.

She sat in the corner between the two houses; it was shaded from the sun and she looked as if she was eating the sweetest cherries in the forest or the richest chocolates in the box.

The smile was back on her face.

'Give me some,' I demanded.

She looked up briefly as she worked on freeing a large piece from her ankle, then concentrated once again as she continued with her task. She smiled as it broke free, leaving a yellow-pink void where the scab had come from. She looked up and grinned as she slipped the piece of crusty scab into her mouth; it was the size of a large coin.

'I will not,' she said. She pointed at my leg as she crunched on the scab. 'You have your own.'

It was true. Only Lasse had not yet developed the horrible scabs. Mama and Karin were the worst, but just recently I had discovered one or two on my arms and one on my ankle bone. I watched as a fly settled on the sore on my ankle and swished it away.

'But you have more and they are thicker and bigger than mine.'

Karin continued chewing and shook her head.

'Please, Karin, give me one of yours. You have lots.'

Karin said nothing.

I never did manage to persuade her to part with any of her crusty dead flesh. As my sores developed I, too, joined in the feast. Karin was right . . . they did taste nice.

CHAPTER 21

The Allotment

~❦~

People were disappearing faster than at any time I could recall in the three camps we had stayed in. Almost daily, women and children simply vanished from 34 Blimbong Street and the other houses. The sight of a handcart covered with a tarpaulin being pushed towards the exit gates was a common sight, so common in fact that it no longer shocked. It was an everyday occurrence . . . normal.

A few days afterwards I would notice new faces walking past our house. Every woman, every child, boy or girl, was a sunken-eyed, stumbling, shuffling bag of bones and many could hardly walk.

Mrs Antje said that even the Japs had not accounted for so many people dying, and there were rumours in the camp at Lampersarie that something would be done and our food rations would be improved. Mrs Antje said that a delegation made up of nurses from the hospital, nuns and some of the leaders of certain houses had approached the commandant of the camp and he had received them very sympathetically. For the first time in a long while there was an air of optimism at number 34 and I even noticed a few of the ladies smiling for a change.

The commandant called a *tenko* late one afternoon and, after we had bowed for several minutes, he appeared in front of the line and allowed us to stand straight.

He announced that fresh green vegetables, radishes, carrots, lettuces and onions would be coming into the camp so that every prisoner would get their fair share of vitamins. We were all so excited and I remember the sensation of my mouth watering naturally by itself, something that I hadn't experienced for a long time. He clapped his hands and one of the soldiers appeared pushing a handcart towards us.

I strained to see what tasty vegetables were on the cart. I was a tantalizing inch or two too short and, as I looked into the faces of the other ladies, I could see they were a little disappointed.

There were no juicy green vegetables on the cart, no onions or radishes to flavour and pack out the cabbage soup. Instead there were bags of seeds and tiny plants no more than an inch or two high.

The commandant walked to the front of the house and marked out a square in the dust. It was no bigger than five by five metres square, and he told us that this was now the communal garden of number 34. It wasn't the communal garden, it was mine. It was only four metres from our blue door; it was the Grønn-Nielsens' garden, we were the keepers . . . it was ours. In those few seconds

I had made my mind up that this garden would be looked after and, because it was so close to our room and our blue door, we would be in charge.

The commandant said we would be given everything needed to cultivate the land and in a few weeks' time we would start to reap the rewards our efforts would bring.

I looked at the ground. It was as hard as a brick but the commandant assured us that, with the right equipment, seeds and plants and plenty of hard work, it would give us everything we needed. A guard reached over the cart and threw down spades, pickaxes and other tools so that we would be able to work the land. He then unloaded the small plants and seeds. He explained that only certain houses had been chosen and we should count ourselves very lucky. I thought about the thousands of poor people sleeping in the barracks with only concrete to look out on to, and thought that this must be what he meant.

I looked across to the other side of the street. We were lucky; not every house had a garden. While many other people looked unhappy, I was smiling and couldn't wait to get started in our new garden. The thought of fresh vegetables was something I could only dream about. The commandant dismissed us and moved on to the next house. As he walked away I looked at Mrs Antje.

'Can we start now?' I asked her.

She gave a big sigh and shrugged her shoulders. 'If you wish, little one. Are you ready for some hard work, because I don't think this ground has seen a spade for one hundred years.'

I nodded and pulled Karin towards me. 'Karin will help, too.'

Mrs Antje laughed. 'We'll need a lot more people to work the land than you two.'

There were no more than half a dozen adults in number 34 who were fit enough to swing a pickaxe and they took turns in five-minute bursts as that was about as much energy as they could spare. The children ferried in tins of water to soften the ground and eventually, after most of the day, Mrs Antje announced that the soil was loose enough to use the spades and trowels. We dug the soil until it was dark and then the next morning, as soon as it was light, we started again. The soil was loose and moist and I begged Mrs Antje to let us begin planting.

She refused.

'The soil must be like a fine powder, free of anything hard.' She told us that today was the day we took out the stones. So we did. We got down on our hands and knees and sifted through the soil, taking out any stone we found. We put them all in a huge pile until we were sure there couldn't be another stone anywhere in sight.

'Are you quite sure there's nothing left?' Mrs Antje asked. We nodded keenly, certain that it would soon be time to sow the seeds and begin planting.

But Mrs Antje made us dig the garden all over again.

We moaned and groaned, but she encouraged us to keep digging.

'Dig for Holland,' she called out. 'Dig for England.' She looked across at me. 'Dig for Norway.'

When we were finished she made us get back down on our hands and knees again to look for stones, and sure enough we found lots.

Mrs Antje returned with a piece of string and we marked out the boundary of the plot. Once that was finished we watered. Thankfully the tap was working that particular day and we poured litres and litres of water onto the land until it resembled a small rice field. Mrs Antje looked on and, if I wasn't mistaken, a slight look of satisfaction flickered across her face.

'It's almost ready,' she announced. 'We must wait until the water soaks in and then we can begin.'

The water took all night to soak in and I hardly slept a wink that night.

I could barely contain my excitement the next day when I woke up and saw the water had gone.

Still she made us dig.

The plot was unrecognizable from what it had been only a few days before. Mrs Antje came from the house with more string and small wooden stakes and we separated the plot into six sections. She showed us how to plant the tiny plants and how to space out the seeds. We finished the garden just as it began to get dark. It was complete and now all we had to do was water and wait. We had parsley, lettuce, carrots, onions and parsnips – I could almost taste each one as we went to bed that evening, exhausted but satisfied with what we had achieved.

I visited Mama whenever she was in hospital and told her all about the progress of the garden . . . my garden. I didn't stray far in the weeks that followed as I was too scared that someone would steal our produce. I set up a watch with the other children so that the garden was never unattended. It was the most amazing thing to see as the plants grew steadily and the shoots from the seeds broke through the surface of the soil. I remember coming out one day when it was very hot and the plants were withered and drooping. I panicked as I thought we had killed them, but one of the ladies told us to give them more water. 'They are thirsty,' she said.

I watched the plants as they began to drink. I watched the tiny leaves like a hawk as they came alive again. I watched for hours, tiny movements, some sudden and some gradual, but all of them noticeable to the naked eye. I called the other children over and we all watched this wonderful act of Mother Nature. Every plant survived.

Mrs Antje showed us how to weed the garden and how to thin out the plants so that they would grow better, thicker and stronger. The parsley was ready first and Mrs Antje allowed the children to take a plant or two each day. I chewed on one of them and broke the other one up into tiny pieces, which we sprinkled on our rice each evening. It was quite incredible the extra flavour it produced.

A few weeks later the leaves of the carrots, onions and parsnips broke the surface and Mrs Antje explained that the heart of the vegetable was growing well under the surface. We watered and weeded and watched and, in time, the lettuce plants developed too. We were all so impatient and begged Mrs Antje to let us dig up the vegetables and eat them. Mrs Antje refused and said the longer we waited the more fresh vegetables there would be.

'It isn't your garden, Lise, remember. The garden is for the whole house.'

Mrs Antje counted everything in the garden and drew up a plan so that each family would get some sort of vegetable. She explained that some plants were growing more quickly than others, but this was good because it meant the harvest would last longer.

Mama had asked to come out of the hospital in time for the day of the first harvest. She was weak, but the nurse said that if she felt up to it she could return to the house, as long as she rested and sat on the blue door during the day.

Mama whispered in my ear as I left. 'Bring me back to the blue door, Lisemor. I miss you all.'

Two days later Karin and I stood on either side of Mama as she lay down on the handcart and was taken back to number 34. Mrs Antje announced that the first of the carrots, onions and parsnips would be ready the following day. The lettuce plants would take a little longer.

Mama had planned our menu. Each family would get half an onion, half a parsnip and a whole carrot. Breakfast would be as normal, porridge, but we would save the rice until evening and have a real feast. We would chop the vegetables finely to be added to the soup and rice – nothing could be boiled as we were not allowed open fires. Mama said that for once Lasse wouldn't get his banana ration; instead it would be cut into four and we would have sweet, too. Mama said one day without a whole banana wouldn't do any harm and, anyway, the extra vegetables he would be getting would more than make up for it.

Several of the ladies were already outside when I walked out to the garden the following morning and I knew something was terribly wrong.

Mrs Antje was standing in the doorway almost in tears.

'What is it?' I asked. 'What is wrong?'

I followed Mrs Antje's eyes and looked at the garden. I walked over and stepped over the boundary string. Normally I would have taken care not to tread on any of the small plants or vegetables, but this time it was not necessary. I fell to my knees as I saw what had been done and, as hard as I tried not to cry, my tears fell onto what was once my beautiful garden.

I sobbed uncontrollably as I asked myself why. By this time Mama had come outside as well and Karin had joined me kneeling in the dirt. She, too, was crying.

The garden had been destroyed.

Everything that had been ready had been stolen during the night. But worse, the small lettuces and tiny plants that hadn't yet developed had been pulled out and scattered everywhere. I picked some of them up and, between the tears, tried to replant them.

Mrs Antje knelt down and told me the roots had been damaged beyond repair and the plants were dead.

We never did find out who had destroyed the garden. At first the atmosphere in the house was very tense as people pointed fingers at certain individuals who had suggested the planned distribution of the food was unfair. I don't think it was anyone at number 34 because I feel sure at least something would have been found. Mrs Antje said it was more likely that it was some of the people from the barracks who were jealous.

'But how can they be jealous?' I asked. 'They have seen how hard we worked.'

Mama sat on the blue door shaking her head and comforting Karin.

The incident was even reported to the commandant and he was very angry and said that no more seeds or plants would be distributed until the culprits had been caught.

The garden was never restored or replanted again.

CHAPTER 22

Bring Me Back to the Blue Door

❧⚜❧

I visited Mama every time she had to go back to the hospital. It was a place of many emotions: I was both scared and yet a little excited each time I entered the building. The hospital was three hundred metres away and I always had to pass the platform to get there.

At first I had imagined that families strolling on the platform were playing some sort of game. They were always watched by the Japanese guards, who seemed more than interested in the people up there.

As I made more trips to the hospital, I asked Mama many questions about what I had witnessed. As a result I now knew the purpose of the platform: it was known in Camp Lampersarie as the punishment block.

The concrete platform was the foundations of a building that had never been finished. The concrete was pale grey, almost white in colour, and as soon as the first rays of early morning sun touched the base it began to bake. It was out in the open with no shade from buildings or trees and it took the full heat of the sun from early morning until last thing at night, when the sun disappeared from sight. It was like a huge communal oven and one boy even told a story of how a Japanese soldier once fried an egg on its surface.

The Japs would place the poor unfortunates on the platform for little or no reason. If a child had been late for *tenko*, showed a lack of respect towards a guard, traded goods at the fence, or had simply been too boisterous, they would be rounded up with their mothers and herded at the point of a bayonet towards the platform.

They begged and cried as they were led up onto its shimmering surface. Within seconds their discomfort became clear. They were always barefoot, and as soon as the skin of their feet touched the concrete they began to burn. Sometimes the Japs would make the poor people kneel and their knees would swell up. It made no difference either way; whichever part of the body came into contact with the concrete, it blistered within a few minutes. In many ways it was like a game to the guards, a game to see how far the prisoners could be pushed, how long it would take until they collapsed or even died. There was always a handcart near the platform and many times I witnessed the body of a lady or small child being pushed away from the platform in the direction of the hospital. I wondered how many made it to the hospital and how many were simply pushed straight to the camp's exit to await collection.

A Japanese guard was positioned at each end of the platform, sitting comfortably under a small shaded bamboo canopy. Each guard would have a bottle of water which would be replenished every hour or so. There was no water and no food for the prisoners on the platform. The guards would watch and shout things at each other, pointing at the desperate plight of the people as they neared collapse. A nurse was sometimes on hand and, as the prisoners fell to the ground, she would be ordered up onto the platform to take them off. She'd bring them to the shade of a tree, give them water to rouse them and bathe their blisters with cool water. The guards would watch carefully until they had regained consciousness, then they would be ordered up on the platform again.

It was a place of indescribable brutality. The torture was left to Mother Nature and the incredible force of the sun. Some guards were extremely cruel. They would watch as children collapsed onto the concrete and refuse to let the nurses tend to them. Then they'd laugh and point at the mothers, crying and begging for their children to be helped.

I never lingered at the platform as Mama always told me to stay away, but I knew some of the families taken to that horrible place, and many of them simply disappeared. Those that survived were never the same again.

Every time Mama was taken away to the hospital, I knew I would have to pass that terrible place, and no matter how many times I tried to look in the other direction as I passed, my curiosity always got the better of me as my eyes scanned the platform for my friends or any of the ladies from number 34 Blimbong Street.

Occasionally my friend Kitty came with me to the hospital, and I always took care to make sure she walked quickly past the platform. Kitty was Dutch and about the same age as me. I first met her when we were on a work detail together.

Mrs Antje came into our room one morning before we were awake. As I woke, Mrs Antje said that I must be part of a young persons' work party. She explained that the work was not difficult and I would be finished in plenty of time to visit Mama later that day in hospital.

'You must come along, too, Karin. It will do you no harm.'

There were about ten of us including Karin, all girls, and Mrs Antje sat me down next to Kitty, who would become one of my best friends. As we sat under the terrace roof of one of the barracks, Kitty smiled and asked me my name. She told me that this was her house; she lived in the big barracks and we were making medicine for the poor people in the hospital. She knew all about the hospital as her sister Marie was a nurse there.

We each got a small thick ceramic bowl and stick. Kitty said it was called a mortar and pestle. Kitty had already reached for the stick and held it in her right fist. A lady brought out a big basket and instructed us to take a little at a time as it would make our task easier.

'A little what?' I asked Kitty.

'Dry bones,' she replied.

'Bones?'

All of a sudden my job had lost any appeal it may have held.

Kitty laughed. 'Don't worry, Lise, they are animal bones and we need to crush them into a powder to make medicine.'

'Animal bones?'

'Yes. Marie told me that there are many animals that die, too, and their bones make fine medicine for the hospital.'

'In what way?' I asked incredulously.

'They sprinkle it on the food. It gives them something called calcium,' she said, shrugging her shoulders.

It was simply the most horrible job.

Hour after hour we pounded and crushed the fragments of bone as best we could. One tiny piece of bone seemed to take forever. I first used my right hand and then the left and then, when I felt that I couldn't crush any more, I would use my right hand again. Every hour we were allowed to stand and were given a little water. A Japanese guard would walk along the line of girls and scowl at us if he thought we weren't working hard enough. Kitty urged me on, saying that if we produced enough powder we would all be rewarded with a spoonful of sugar.

A spoonful of sugar seemed scant reward for this many hours of work and by now I had two blisters on the palm of each hand. My big reward was the new friendship I had found with Kitty. Poor Karin returned exhausted that evening with big open blisters on the palms of her hand and Mrs Antje said she would not have to return.

Kitty came to the hospital with me more often than Karin and Lasse. Kitty's mama was not in hospital, but she was allowed to visit her sister more or less anytime she wanted and would help serve the food and medicines. Lasse was never strong enough to make the long walk to the hospital in the heat and much preferred to sleep. There was no shade anywhere en route and one of the Dutch ladies was always happy to take care of him. Karin, too, preferred to sit in the shade of the tree on the blue door.

I sat with Mama on her bed for many hours and she would ask about Karin and Lasse, the food and the sores and our dysentery, and every time I told her that things were fine.

She would get worried about my pilfering and told me that, if I were caught, the Nips would punish both of us. They seldom punished the smaller children, she said, only the mothers. We would all end up on the platform.

'Please do not steal anything, Lisemor,' she begged.

The platform scared me and I knew that Mama was in no condition to be sent there. As always I gave her the answer she was looking for: I promised her I would not steal again.

I lied.

By now I had come to realize that if I couldn't steal those little extras that were so important we would most likely die anyway. I stole to survive.

I'd ask Mama about the small tin plates filled with water that each leg of her bed sat in. Mama laughed and said they were swimming pools for the ants so they could enjoy a swim, but I knew they were filled with a kind of bleach that killed the ants as they attempted to crawl up the legs of the bed.

The hospital was an exciting and calm place; it was like a

different world to the harsh, brutal conditions outside. There were no Japanese guards or officials in the hospital and the nurses were beautifully presented in clean cotton dresses. I thought this most strange and wondered where the clothes came from and where they were washed. The food was a little better in the hospital and the nurses brought it round on trolleys. Mama would try and get me to eat some of the food, but I always refused. I knew that the food in there made her better, and the more she ate the sooner she would be able to join us on the blue door.

This was a familiar pattern.

Mama would deteriorate and end up in hospital. In hospital, with proper care and attention and a better diet, she grew stronger and it was as if her diseases miraculously disappeared. Once outside again in the dirty, cramped, damp conditions of the storeroom, and with an almost non-existent diet, the diseases would return until she was so weak she couldn't stand. Mrs Antje would check on her daily and then announce it was back to hospital again.

Each time Mama went into hospital I wondered if she would make it back out. Even at such a young age I knew that anyone who went into hospital had to be very ill indeed, and more people disappeared from the hospital than anywhere else. I sat with Mama once and made a passing comment about her legs. They were all fat and swollen and pink. Mama told me to press a finger on her leg. At first I refused, but it was as if Mama was playing a practical joke.

'Do it,' Mama said. 'See what happens.'

So I did. I pressed my finger into her leg and it sank in as easy as pushing your finger into cake mixture.

'A little further,' she said.

It was a weird experience, but I did as she asked and pushed my finger in right up to the knuckle. When I withdrew my finger the hole in Mama's leg did not move and where my finger had been was all white.

'See, Lisemor,' she said. 'I have a magic leg.'

I watched carefully as, ever so slowly, the blood flowed into the indentation again and the hole in her leg closed.

'What is it, Mama?' I asked.

Mama sighed. 'It is the beriberi, Lisemor.'

Kitty and I could never resist exploring whenever we went up to the hospital together. I remember one occasion in particular, when Kitty returned and told me all about the death room. Kitty explained about each ward; she claimed her sister had told her about the different wards and the room at the end of the long corridor where no one wanted to end up.

Mama was in a room with eighteen other ladies and I thought the level of care was very good. However, Kitty explained that there were smaller wards in the hospital, some with only twelve beds, where, because they were much worse, the patients were looked after even better and got more food and medicine. The nurses visited them every hour to check on their condition. If they improved they were put back into the bigger ward and if they deteriorated they were put into another room where there were only six beds and nurses were constantly on hand. Kitty looked at me and frowned. 'Then there is the death room,' she said.

The death room had four beds. The patients were moved there to die, she explained. I'll never forget her face as she told me all about the death room and said we must never let Mama go in there.

On the way out Kitty led me by the hand and walked me right to the end of the corridor. She pointed at a door to the right, taking care not to go too near, as if we were in danger of catching something from within. She edged ever closer and whispered as she pointed her finger.

'That's it, Lise, the room of death.' She turned to face me, her eyes wide open. 'No one ever comes out of there alive.'

Just then the door to the death room swung open and a nurse wearing a dark-blue apron came through carrying a small black case. She looked at us with a frown and beckoned with a thin, bony finger for us to come forward. We screamed in unison and ran all the way down the corridor and out into the sunshine. We didn't look back until we were sitting on the blue door.

Now I knew that everything Kitty had told me about the death room was true.

CHAPTER 23

Yeast Cakes and Cod Liver Oil

❧

Mama was not in her normal bed when I returned the following day. I asked one of the nurses where she was, a little panicky after what Kitty had told me about the death room.

'She's been moved, darling,' she explained and pointed down the corridor. My heart was in my mouth; I could barely speak. The nurse must have seen the look of horror on my face and took me by the hand.

'Don't worry,' she said, 'we have simply moved her somewhere where she will be looked after a little better.'

It was true, I thought . . . Kitty had been right: she was being moved to a ward with fewer beds and more nurses. The nurse led me down the corridor and my eyes fixed on the room at the end.

No, I thought to myself, not that room. Please God, don't let Mama be in there.

The nurse stopped and pointed into a room well before we got anywhere near the death room.

'There she is, darling,' she said.

Mama was lying on her side, fast asleep. She didn't look too well, but I was just relieved that she was alive and nowhere near that horrible place at the end of the corridor.

I sat with Mama for over an hour before she woke up. She was very weak but lied and told me she felt just fine.

'They have moved me into this room so I get a little more medicine, Lisemor,' she explained.

I visited her every day and thankfully she did improve. She told me that she was getting yeast cakes every day to fight the beriberi.

'The yeast cakes are beautiful,' she said, 'and every time I eat one my strength returns.'

'Then why don't you eat fifty?' I asked.

'Ah, Lisemor,' Mama laughed. 'If only it were that easy. They give me all they can – one a day if I'm lucky, occasionally two.'

I asked Mama what the yeast cakes looked like and she explained that they were a similar size to the small sweet oat biscuits we used to get in Surabaya, but a little thicker.

A nurse wandered into Mama's room pushing a shiny steel trolley. It looked so clean and free of dust and grime that it seemed out of place in the rest of our world. The nurse was clean, too, and tidy in her crisp white blouse. She smiled at me and then went to attend to a patient across the other side of the room. Mama explained that the patient was not well at all.

'Will she die?' I asked.

'Perhaps,' Mama said, 'perhaps. Only God knows.'

'Will they move her to the death room?' I asked.

Mama asked me what I meant by the death room, and I explained what Kitty had told me and about the nurse in the dark uniform. Mama seemed to choke up a little and I noticed a tear or two in her eyes. She said we mustn't call the room that awful name and yet she knew exactly which room I was referring to.

'But, Mama,' I said, 'that's the room—'

'Shhh,' she said, holding up her hand and placing a finger to her lips. 'Didn't you hear? I don't want to talk about it.'

And when Mama looked like that it really was the end of the discussion.

Now my attention was focused on something else. I was looking underneath the trolley at a large silver tin. The tin had been covered by a white cloth that had only just slipped to the bottom of the trolley. It was the movement of the cloth falling that had caught my eye. I edged forward and bent down a little, trying to see what was inside the tin.

'What are you doing, Lisemor?' Mama asked.

I pointed at the tin and the biscuit-like shapes inside. Mama leant across the bed. She smiled. 'Yeast cakes, Lisemor. They make me better.'

'Can I take one?' I asked.

Mama's eyes widened in horror. 'No, Lisemor, you mustn't. You mustn't touch the cakes.'

I didn't want to defy Mama, really I didn't, but I thought back to when she had described the cakes and how tasty they were and how good they were for you and I just couldn't stop myself.

'No,' Mama said, 'please no . . .'

I had one eye on the cakes and the other on the nurse, who was still busy with the unwell patient. My hand slipped into the tin and I felt it close around two of the shapes. I focused on the nurse as I lifted them clear of the tin. I stood up and slipped one of the cakes into my mouth. It melted as soon as it touched my tongue and the beautiful sweet taste seemed to explode all around my mouth. I closed my eyes and it took all of my will-power not to moan out loud in ecstasy. I could still hear Mama scolding me and, when I opened my eyes, the nurse was on her way back over to the trolley with her eyes fixed firmly on me.

I swallowed hard as she spoke to me. 'Now then, little lady, and what are you up to?'

I was gripped with fear as I thought about what the Japs might do to me or Mama. I shook my head, but did not speak in case the nurse saw any trace of crumbs on my lips or in my mouth. She leaned forward and for a second I thought she was going to grab me and take me to the Japs. If she counted the cakes she would know that there were two missing. She reached down, felt inside the tin and pulled out a yeast cake. She held it out in front of me.

'Do you know what these are, young lady?'

I shook my head.

'They are yeast cakes. And do you know how special they are?'

I shook my head. She must have seen me, I thought.

She reached forward and ruffled my hair, then she spoke.

'And they are going to make your Mama all better.' She

leaned over and whispered, 'But for now she must rest. Give your Mama a nice big kiss now and run along.'

I couldn't kiss Mama quickly enough and I almost ran down the corridor. I thought about keeping the remaining yeast cake for Karin and Lasse, but the fear of the nurse counting the cakes and running after me was too great, so I popped it in my mouth and by the time I reached the door at the end of the corridor it had gone.

I had destroyed the evidence.

Only then did I begin to breathe normally again.

Karin was sitting on the blue door when I got back to the house. I was just about to tell her all about the delicious yeast cakes when I thought better of it. And as I stared at her thin skeletal figure, the ribs sticking out of her chest and the sharp bony points of her shoulders, an enormous guilt washed over me. I felt so bad that I hadn't saved even a small portion for my sister.

Just when I thought it couldn't get any worse, the monsoon rains started again. There was water everywhere: it came through the roof, windows and doors and onto the floor where we slept. Mrs Antje and Jolien invited us to sit on their makeshift beds at times, to wait for the rain to stop. Lasse and Karin loved it, and cuddled up close to these lovely ladies, but big sister had to sweep out the slush and clean up the mess in our storeroom. There was nowhere to sleep until it got dry, so we had to bed down on dry floor somewhere else in the house. During those awful days I was happy that Mama was in a hospital bed and off the ground.

The air and surroundings became lovely and fresh after the rain, but while it poured I was reminded of the horrible rain-soaked, stinking garage at the Wijk camp.

The garden at the back of the house looked like a swimming pool and the streets turned into rivers. Everything became wet and, to get out of the water, we had to take refuge on the blue door. The humidity gave us rashes and festering wounds. We children made the best of it and ran around in the rain and mud. It made our wounds worse and they became infected, but it didn't stop us. One of the nurses had some cream and she patched us up as best she could. She had one small tube, which she used up in less than half an hour. She went back to the hospital to ask for some more, but there was none. Karin and I talked with the ladies of the happy times we'd had in Bergen, when nobody took any notice of the rain, they just wrapped up well and grabbed an umbrella. Grandma always told us, 'There is no such thing as bad weather, only bad clothes.' Mrs Antje and the other ladies came from Holland and Belgium and suffered the same weather conditions as people from Bergen.

The monsoon rain was terrible for those who were working in the camp kitchens as there was only a small corrugated iron roof to give a little shelter. With all the rain and strong winds, the fires under the large pots went out all the time. The poor ladies worked like mad to keep the flames going. I remember seeing them standing up to their ankles in mud, wafting at the flames with pieces of cardboard. Sometimes it worked, but more often than not the fires went out and then there was no food for anyone.

During the monsoon I began to take notice of the large pots they cooked the rice in. They were normally taken away when they could scrape no more rice from the bottom. One day I peered into one of the pots and was surprised to see a layer of rice encrusted on the bottom.

As I walked away I concocted a plan. This was good food; why wasn't anyone getting the rice on the bottom? I could only think that the pots were too deep for the ladies to reach into. I found a box to stand on and a stick, then I took a quick look around to make sure none of the other children had noticed me before I climbed over the edge and jumped into the pot. I crouched down for a few seconds and waited. It was all quiet. No one had seen me. I was in food heaven and congratulated myself that my plan had worked. The rice on the bottom was burned black, having been cooked over an open fire for at least an hour, but as I scraped a little off and ate it, I was pleasantly surprised at how good it tasted. I licked my lips; in fact it tasted a whole lot better than the tasteless concoction we had been given as our rations.

I scraped and scraped with the stick for ten minutes and got just about enough to fill two pockets. Then I sat down and filled my stomach. When I could eat no more, I decided it was time to make my escape. I tried to climb over the edge of the huge pot, but it was not easy; the sides were slippery, so I was unable to get a grip with my feet. The only way out was to pull myself up using my arms. I tried unsuccessfully three or four times but did not have enough strength. My muscles were wasted, and each time I tried they grew weaker and weaker. I felt panicky, my heart was beating fast, and I wondered if I should call for help. I decided not to as I was worried I might get punished. I sat in the pot for several minutes thinking about what to do. All was quiet; everyone had vacated the kitchen area. There was only one way out. I started throwing myself against the sides of the pot. The bottom of the pot was slightly rounded and after three or four goes it began to wobble. I threw myself as hard as I could against one side and then the other and eventually I began to get some momentum going. Finally the pot fell over and I spilled out onto the dirt. I looked up at several groups of ladies in the distance. Luckily nobody seemed to have noticed and I ran away as fast as my legs could carry me.

Mama was not very pleased when I presented her with the rice and told her where it had come from. She thought I had been stealing again and worried about how I could have been punished.

'But I did not steal from anyone,' I told her. 'The rice would have been washed away anyway.'

I'm not sure she was totally convinced, but she seemed to enjoy the extra rice I had brought for her.

CHAPTER 24

The Boy in a Cotton Dress

❧❧

I came across him one day as I went to the toilet. It was a most peculiar sight. He had left the door ajar and I couldn't help noticing that he was standing up and peeing like a boy, and yet he wore a dress.

'What are you doing?' I asked.

He got a real fright and shouted at me for watching him.

'You shouldn't leave the door open then,' I answered.

'And you should mind your own business.'

I studied him carefully as he finished and tried to push past me. His hair was long and blond and brushed over his face, but it was clear he was a boy of about eleven years old.

'Why are you wearing a dress?' I called after him.

He turned round and put his finger to his lips, 'Shhhhh,' he said. 'Someone will hear, someone will find out.'

He held out his hand and introduced himself in a whisper. 'Mama said you must call me Petra, but my real name is Pieter.'

Pieter explained that his mama was very scared that he would be sent away to the men's camps and, for the whole year they had been imprisoned at Lampersarie, she had hidden him away in the house and only allowed him out after dark and in a dress.

I asked about *tenko* and he explained that he always stood in the back row so the Japanese would not suspect anything. His mama had pointed out the spelling mistake on the paperwork and changed Pieter to Petra. He said that the stupid Japs simply changed it and that they all believed he was a girl.

I told him they would soon find out the truth if they saw him peeing like I had.

'You are right,' he said. 'I must learn to be more careful.'

Pieter always wore the cotton dress and his mama patched it up with anything she could find until it looked like one of the quilts we had had on our bed in Surabaya. Pieter and I became great friends. As darkness drew in each evening, Pieter came calling for me. We would shin up the tree next to the blue door and sit on the roof overlooking the camp. If we spotted any Japs, we would simply lie flat on the roof and become invisible. Pieter would bring books up onto the roof and we would read in the evenings when the moon was at its fullest. We would also write and draw on pieces of paper or cardboard he'd managed to find in the house. Pieter was very sad that he was never allowed out during the day, but we made the most of our nights on the roof. It was a truly special place as Karin did not have the strength to climb the tree. We scratched our names onto the tiles on the roof and Pieter lodged a cardboard notice stating 'Private' between two of the slates.

I sat on the roof one night waiting for Pieter, and as usual the poor old tree creaked alarmingly as his thin arms and legs struggled to make it up onto the rooftop. I tried to pull up this weak and starving friend with my last ounce of strength, until we both nearly fell off the roof in a fit of giggles. Then I noticed he was wearing shorts and asked him why.

'My mama wanted to do some laundry this evening, since we seem to get water more frequently these days,' he replied.

It was true. Getting more water was one of the changes we had noticed lately; I also couldn't remember our last *tenko*, or the last time I'd seen a beating. Still, Pieter not wearing his dress was scary, and I made him promise to put it on the next day, even if the Japs seemed more relaxed around us. It made my skin crawl just thinking what they would do to him if they found out he was a boy and not a girl.

CHAPTER 25

Christmas 1944

❧❧❧

From the first day in camp we had been eating our food from the lids of tins we had been given by Mrs Antje. The lids had no depth, and more often than not the food spilled onto the ground. We were so hungry that we would scrape it up and eat the food along with the dirt, sand and any insects or bugs nearby. I hated those damned lids, even though Mama told us to pretend that they were the finest china.

Now, as I left the hospital after visiting Mama, I spied a golden opportunity, a chance to throw away those lids forever. The plates sat on top of a trolley, which was similar to the one I had pilfered the yeast cakes from, only this one was right by the door that led outside. There were two nurses in the corridor standing by the trolley and I pretended to look into the other wards as I played for a little time. The nurses were always busy, always overworked, and I knew that if I hung around long enough they would leave.

I was right.

Within two minutes I heard their conversation coming to an end. I walked slowly towards them. I timed it to perfection. When I was about five metres away, I ran forward, lifted up the plates and pushed them under my blouse. I opened the door to the outside and took a quick look to make sure there were no Japs. I took a few seconds to catch my breath and then walked slowly back to our storeroom at number 34 Blimbong Street.

I wouldn't let Karin or Lasse eat off the china plates until Mama made it back from the hospital. It was a surprise for her and, even though I think she knew where they had come from, she didn't say anything. No food fell onto the floor that night. Mama and Lasse ate from the plates first and then Karin and I ate from them afterwards. It was strange and made no sense, but somehow the bland food tasted better. Those plates were so very special to me.

The following day I was determined to put some real food onto those beautiful plates. I had discussed my mission with one of the boys in the house and we knew exactly where to go. The waste water from the kitchen areas spilled out at the bottom end of the camp under a bridge and flowed into a natural brook on the other side of the fence. The water on the other side flowed fast. On days when it was particularly hot and dusty, I longed to take off all of my clothes and immerse myself in the cool water, but it was never to be. I stood and stared at that stream for hours. Sadly, on our side of the fence, the muddy pool was stagnant and filthy, but nevertheless that's where the eels lived.

'You are sure the meat is tasty?'

Rayan nodded. 'Yes, my mama caught a big one here once and killed it and grilled it on a stick above a fire.'

He licked his lips and rubbed his stomach. 'It was beautiful.'

Rayan had brought the matches and collected the wood we would use for cooking them. I had brought the knife and the big sticks to hit them with.

'Okay, here goes,' I said and we waded into the mud bare-footed.

I held Rayan's hand, a bit for balance and a bit for comfort.

I held a stick in the other hand high above my head, poised and at the ready.

'Aim for their heads,' he said. 'That stuns them, then you can hit them as many times as you like until they are dead.'

'Won't the eels get angry?' I asked.

'Oh yes,' he replied.

'So they will try and bite us?'

'Yes.' He grinned. 'But we will be too quick for them and enjoy our grilled Christmas supper tonight.' At the time I did not know the difference between eels and snakes.

I remembered my mother's warnings back in Surabaya about the poisonous snakes that would kill us if they bit us. She told us about pythons, elephant trunk snakes, dog-faced snakes and wart snakes, and here I was wading through the mud with my Dutch friend so that we could deliberately disturb and annoy them before battering them with sticks. I knew it was dangerous, so did Rayan, but the empty feeling in my stomach told me it was worth the risk when I envisaged the hot steaming meat covering the surface of my china plates.

'There's one!' Rayan shouted suddenly, and I looked over to where he was pointing. Sliding quickly from the other end of the pond was an almost black eel with a lighter-coloured head. It was nearly one metre in length and covered in mud. We launched ourselves at it, swinging wildly with our sticks, but it was far too quick for us and within an instant it had disappeared. We spent most of the day in that horrible stinking pool and managed to disturb and annoy four or five eels but never caught any. The nearest we got was trapping a huge specimen between two big rocks. I approached it with my stick high above my head, ready to hit it, then it sprang forward in a threatening manner as if to say: any nearer and I will get you. I looked at Rayan and he looked at me. Between us we agreed that we weren't that hungry anyway and slowly edged away to the relative safety of the camp.

It was Christmas Day 1944 and we were all sitting on our blankets on the blue door. There were no presents or special dinners, but we were on the blue door with Mama and she was telling us tales from back home in Norway. She told us how the snow would have been on the ground for many weeks in Bergen and that the children would be making snowmen and throwing snowballs. Karin and I still remembered that wonderful holiday in Norway before the war started and, as I sat in the baking Javan heat, Mama mentioned one of the special days: Papa's birthday on 9 April. Her face looked sad for a second when she mentioned that 9 April was also the day when Germany invaded Norway. She moved on quickly to 17 May.

'Norwegian National Day,' she announced proudly. She was smiling. 'My birthday,' she said. 'Just wait till we get back to Norway. We can celebrate every day as if it's Norwegian National Day.'

'What will we eat, Mama?' Karin asked.

'We will eat anything we want, my darling. We will have sausages and potatoes, cakes and custard, jelly and ice cream, and we will have chocolate and sweets and oranges and apples and nuts.'

I had forgotten what those things tasted like. Lasse and Karin were smiling as Mama told her happy tales, but I didn't think mentioning all that food was such a good idea.

It wasn't long before Mama was back in hospital. It was happening too often and I was very worried. I was even more worried when I went to visit her as she had been put straight into the intensive care room with only six beds and nurses constantly on duty. Mama looked terrible; her legs were so swollen and hard that I could no longer push my finger into them and she seemed to be almost permanently asleep. It was boring when Mama slept. I liked talking to her and telling her about Lasse and Karin. I looked around the room. It was small and there were no trolleys to search; a nurse was sitting on a seat in the corner reading charts. I decided to have a walk outside. I started walking around the perimeter of the hospital. I thought that if I walked around twelve times, then went back into Mama's room, she might be awake. I had walked around six times when I turned the corner and spotted two of the nurses who had wandered outside. They were sharing a cigarette and talking and I could overhear what they were saying. I took a couple of steps back around the corner and sat down to listen.

'How is your department today?' one of them asked.

Her friend replied that it was very bad. Then, to my horror, she said, 'Today I helped two of them to heaven.'

I put my hand over my mouth as I remembered that I had seen one of them coming from the death room.

I ran back to Mama's room, but still she slept. I prayed that Mama would never end up in that room with the nurse who helped people get to heaven.

Two days later my worst nightmare came true.

There were more people on the platform as I passed en route to the hospital. Three families, three mamas, two boys and a girl of no more than seven years old, who was squatting on the hot surface, crying and clinging to her mama's legs. Two Japs stood under a canopy with bottles of water on a table next to them. The heat was sweltering and I could feel the perspiration running down my back as I passed them. A nurse stood under a tree looking on anxiously. Nothing had changed and I so wanted to help, but there was nothing I could do. I did as Mama instructed and hurried past, turning my face away. Everyone who walked by turned their faces away, pleased it was not them or their family being punished, slowly being boiled to the point of death.

When I arrived at the hospital, Mama was not in the room where I had last visited her. I didn't panic too much as I recalled the last time she had been moved, when I had felt a bit silly panicking over nothing. Perhaps she had got a little better and been moved to the big ward. Yes, that's it, her yeast cakes had worked and she was getting better. I walked into the big ward with a smile on my face as my eyes searched the room. The smile quickly disappeared as I looked at the thin, drawn patients. I looked at each bed, staring into the sunken eyes of people who stared back at me. Some of them had a yellow tinge, some had sores around their mouths and where their hairline started, and they all lay still. I looked again but could not see Mama. I checked each bed a second time to see if I'd missed her. There was a lady on the far side whose face I could not see as she lay on her side facing the wall. As I walked over I recognized her blond hair, albeit thin and in need of a good wash.

'Mama,' I called out as I reached her. 'It is me, Lisemor.' I shook her by the shoulder and she woke and turned over.

It was not Mama.

I checked the other wards, too, and she was not there, but I could not bring myself to walk down to the death room.

A nurse found me crying in the corridor and asked me what was wrong. Between sobs I managed to blurt out my fear that Mama must be in the death room as I couldn't find her anywhere else.

The nurse took me by the hand and said, 'Let's take a look.'

It was the longest walk of my life as she led me slowly to the end of the corridor. As we approached the room I peered round the corner. Before I even spotted her the nurse had pointed into the far corner. 'There she is, darling, there's Mama.'

Mama was sleeping. She looked awful, far worse than I had ever seen her before, and although I shook her several times she would not wake up.

'Let her rest,' the nurse said. 'She has just had some food and you must let her sleep.'

I didn't want Mama to sleep. I was shaking my head. Mama was not going to wake up. Mama was in the death room and she was going to die. I sat with her for hours before she woke up. She was so weak she could barely speak, but even so she managed a little smile when she realized I was at her bedside. Mama went back to sleep almost straightaway and I decided it would be better not to wake her again. I walked over to the nurse who had brought me in.

'Is Mama going to die?' I asked.

The nurse looked me in the eye and I could tell that she didn't have the answer I was looking for.

'She is very weak,' she replied. 'She has yellow fever and beri-beri, but she is being well fed and we have some medicines and yeast cakes for her. She has even had some cod liver oil from her doctor friend.'

'Then why is she in the death room?' I asked. 'People who come in here die, Kitty says.'

'And who is Kitty, darling?'

'My friend.'

'And how old is Kitty?'

'Eleven.'

The nurse smiled. 'Then she does not know the ways of the world.'

'Then who does? I asked you if Mama is going to live or die. Surely you should know that.'

The nurse stood up and led me once again by the hand. Her hand felt warm and comforting. She spoke. 'There is only one person who knows, little one, and that is the Lord Almighty.'

'Who?'

'God,' she answered.

Not him again, I thought.

'But can't you help my mama to live? And why have you put her in the death room and why have—?'

The nurse put a finger to her lips and stopped me.

'Please do not call it the death room.'

'But—'

'It is true that many of the people in this ward will not live because they are so ill, but they are in here so that we can watch them every minute of the day. They get the best medicines and the best food.' She looked into the ward again. 'Well, some of them do anyway.'

I didn't understand. 'What do you mean?' I asked.

'Nothing,' she said quickly.

'Please tell me,' I cried, tugging at her skirt.

She looked up and down the corridor.

'Follow me,' she instructed.

I walked outside with her and she turned to face me. She bent down so that her eyes looked straight into mine. 'You are right,' she said. 'Even we nurses call it the death room. Some of the ladies in there will not make it, and we know exactly who they are, so we give the medicines to those we think have a chance.'

She was smiling as she spoke. 'Your mama is getting the medicine, little one, because we think she has a chance, but you must realize how ill she is.'

I found myself nodding as I fought hard to control the tears that seemed to have been falling more easily and frequently over the past few weeks. The nurse was cuddling me and telling me to be brave, but I could see tears in her eyes as well.

'You must believe that your mama will come out of that room,' she said. 'You must believe she will get better and you must believe that the Japanese will lose this war. If you really believe then it will happen.'

She held me at arm's length and spoke again. 'You want to believe, don't you?'

'Yes,' I sniffed.

'Then go home and tell your sister that Mama is ill but she will get better.'

As I walked off, the nurse called after me to give Mama a few days' rest and then to come back with Karin.

I found Karin walking through the house towards the blue door with Lasse, carrying the china plates. They were dripping with water; it appeared she had been washing them under the tap in the back garden area.

I took a deep breath as I prepared my speech to tell her about Mama and the death room and how we must all believe really, really hard that she would pull through and that everything would be okay. We would win the war and get out of this horrible place quickly.

Then, to my horror, Karin's leg slipped out from underneath her on the wet tiles in front of our room and she fell to the ground in a heap. I watched in slow motion as my beautiful china dishes seemed to hang in the air. Then, in an instant, they crashed to the ground and smashed into a thousand pieces.

My carefully planned speech did not come. Instead I shouted at my sister and told her how stupid she was. I shouted at her so much that she climbed the tree beside the blue door for the first time and sat sobbing on the roof, refusing to come down.

It was at least two hours before I was able to tell my sister about the war and how we would all be leaving the camp at Lampersarie soon.

Karin was obviously very concerned about Mama being in the death room and two days later she walked with me to the hospital. It was an enormous effort for her and during the long walk I was sure she would not make it. We paused several times as she took a rest. We rested at the platform, and it was there that I took a good look at her poor legs. No wonder she could hardly walk: her legs were as thin as the bamboo poles that supported the fences. I suggested she go back to the blue door, but no, she insisted she wanted to see Mama.

Eventually, after what seemed like forever, we reached the entrance to the hospital. We were stopped by a nice female doctor who asked why we were there. I explained that we were visiting Mama and she smiled. However, she asked if she could take Karin away and examine her. Karin shrugged her shoulders. I pushed her along behind the doctor, who took her into a small side room.

I slid down the wall and waited for her.

Karin appeared after just a few minutes with a grin on her face.

'What is it?' I asked. 'Why are you so happy?'

She shook her head and told me she needed to go to the toilet.

I waited for five minutes before she reappeared. She was rubbing her stomach and smiling. She took a quick look up and down the corridor and told me the doctor had given her two tomatoes.

'She told me I needed the vitamins but made me go into the toilets to eat them in secret.'

'Didn't you think to give me one?' I asked.

Karin shook her head. 'The doctor said I mustn't. They were for me because of the scabs on my legs and my mouth ulcers.'

I could not get angry as I remembered the yeast cakes and how I hadn't given my sister or little brother a second thought when I'd crammed them into my mouth as quickly as I could. Karin had felt exactly the same: those tomatoes were the most important thing in her life at the moment the doctor handed them over. She hadn't thought of me or Lasse, not even Mama. I cursed the Japs for what they were doing to us.

*

Oh, what joy!

Mama was out of the horrible death room. I confess it was one of the most wonderful moments during our time in any of those awful camps. I had been convinced that Mama was near to death and that, once she had been taken into that room, there would be no turning back. We sat on either side of her bed and she told us how much better she was feeling and that the extra food she had been getting was helping her to grow stronger every day. As we left the ward she called after us that she would be back on the blue door in a few days. Mama's spirits were high. I think she, too, had been scared of that room and was happy to be leaving it at long last.

As we walked down a corridor, the doctor who had given Karin the tomatoes stood with a nurse who was crying. She was trying to comfort her and had her arms round the nurse's shoulders as she sobbed. I told Karin not to stop; perhaps one of her patients had died. As we passed the nurse I heard what was wrong. The nurse was crying because she had no medicine to give her patients. She was explaining to the doctor that the diseases were easy to treat with the right medicine but, no matter how many times she asked the Japs and how many times they wrote her instructions down, the medicine never arrived.

The poor nurse cried about patients dying every day and, although the doctor reassured and comforted her, I looked into her eyes and realized that she too felt helpless.

I heard the handcart before I actually saw it. Karin and I were on the blue door and Lasse was sleeping under the tree on a blanket. The cart wheel squeaked terribly and, as it came closer, I put my hands over my ears.

'Lisemor,' a voice called, 'Karin . . . Lasse . . .'

It was Mama on the cart; she was out of hospital. I jumped up and ran to greet her. Karin followed slowly and Lasse stirred from his afternoon nap. The two ladies pushing the cart helped her down and lowered her onto the door before handing her a little bundle. I could see that Mama had used a lot of energy just getting down from the cart, but her face was rosy red with colour and she was smiling, glad to be back.

She took her bundle from the ladies. 'A little more food for me, Lisemor, then a good night's sleep and I'll be as good as new.'

I smiled and hugged Mama tightly, but I knew she would never be good as new again.

It was still dark when I heard the sound of *tenko*. Mama groaned. 'Lisemor,' she said, 'quickly, take Karin and Lasse and do as they say.'

'*Tenko, tenko*,' the guards shouted as they worked the siren. This was not a normal *tenko*: the Japs sounded angry.

'But, Mama,' I begged as I roused Karin from a deep sleep, 'you must come, too.'

Mama sighed. 'I am afraid that is not possible, Lisemor. My legs will not carry me outside. I cannot even stand up straight.'

'Then what will you do?' I asked. 'The Japs will be looking and—'

'Hush, Lisemor, they will think I am still in hospital. Now go quickly.'

I managed to bundle Karin and Lasse outside and we stood in line with the rest of the families. The Japs were rushing around looking very agitated. At first I breathed a sigh of relief as they did not seem interested in our names or numbers, but my heart almost stopped beating as one of them ran down and through the door of our house.

'No,' I wanted to shout at them, 'please leave Mama alone.' Then I heard her. Mama was pleading and begging with the guard. She was telling him she was ill, that she couldn't walk. I heard him growl and then I heard him strike her and a muffled cry. I wanted to close my eyes and cover my ears with my hands. He was shouting, '*Tenko, tenko,*' and Mama was crying out in pain. I could only imagine the scene that was taking place behind the wall.

The commotion continued and then I spotted the guard coming outside. I strained to look for Mama and became aware of the guard dragging something behind him.

It was Mama.

He was still shouting and dragging her by the arm.

'Walk,' he ordered. 'Walk now.'

Mama was sobbing uncontrollably and trying her best to get to her feet. Her legs were swollen and had an angry red colour. I wanted to shout at the horrible man and tell him how ill she was. I fought my tears as he dragged her towards the line. He lifted her physically to her feet and one of the other ladies tried to support her. I could see in her face that she was trying her hardest to stand. Her eyes were screwed tight shut and she grimaced in pain. It was then I realized that her legs were swollen to twice their normal size and yellow pus poured out of the sores like lard.

It was all too much for her and she collapsed in a heap at the guard's feet. Only then did he realize she was telling the truth. He looked at her crying on the ground, shouted something in Japanese, kicked her once and walked away.

Another guard told her not to move and instructed no one to help her, then they walked away. The Japs searched several houses, looking for something or someone. For a second I thought they might be looking for Pieter and I gazed along the line. I caught my breath as I spied the dirty white cotton dress fluttering in the breeze and his long blond hair covering his face. Thank goodness for small mercies.

The Japs found nothing. Mrs Antje told me they were looking for valuables – money and jewellery.

The next morning a handcart appeared at the door and Mama was loaded onto it for a quick return to hospital. As two of the ladies pushed it away, Mama was upset and apologized to us.

'I will be back soon,' she said. 'Don't worry, my little ones. Lisemor,' she said, 'take care of your brother and sister and come and see me tomorrow. I have something to tell you.'

As I watched the cart trundle away, I wondered how long Mama had to live and prayed that this awful war would end. It had to end . . . it needed to end or Mama would not make it.

She was very weak and lethargic when I went to see her the

following day. She held my hand throughout the visit. I did not look for yeast cakes or tomatoes or for anything to pilfer. I looked into the desperate eyes of my mama as she told me about a chest of drawers and how I must take care of everything. I looked into the eyes of a lady without hope.

She explained about the chest of drawers in our room back at number 34 Blimbong Street. 'There is an envelope taped to the back. Leave it where it is for the moment as the Japs have not found it up to now.'

I found myself nodding my head. 'There are American dollars in it; this is the money you need to help you survive after the war. And in the flaps of your rucksacks, too: there are a few dollars more in there.'

'But, Mama,' I said, 'why are you telling me this? You will be with us after the war; we will all survive. We will leave here together and go to Norway and—'

'No, Lisemor, listen to me!' she interrupted. She was breathing heavily and I could tell that her very important talk to me was draining her of energy. 'Please,' she scolded, 'listen and do as I say.'

'But, Mama, I—'

'Lisemor, the dollars, remember where they are, and look after your brother and sister, and don't forget to ask Mrs Antje and Jolien for help.'

'No, Mama,' I said, 'I'm not listening. I—'

This time it was an English nurse who interrupted. She took me by the hand. 'I think your mother needs to sleep, my darling.'

I looked into Mama's eyes. They were filled with tears again. Before I could say anything or object, Mama sighed and closed her eyes.

'C'mon, darling, she needs to rest.' Reluctantly I walked off with the nurse and she led me outside.

'Give her a few days and I will build her up again. She is not strong.'

'You'll give her medicine?' I asked.

'Yes.'

'And yeast cakes?'

'And yeast cakes.'

'And tomatoes?'

'And cod liver oil?'

She placed a finger over my lips. 'I will give her everything she needs.'

'And you won't send her to the death room?'

The kind nurse smiled. 'Cross my heart and hope to die.' She made the sign of the cross on her shirt and pushed me gently on my way.

'Go now,' she insisted. 'I heard your mother: you have a brother and sister to look after.'

I walked away, wondering what she meant by crossing her heart and hoping to die.

CHAPTER 26

A Women's Working Party and One Small Girl

❦

I hated it when Mama was in hospital and was constantly on the lookout for something to do to keep my mind occupied. I longed to leave the compound that had been such a huge part of my life and constantly envied the working parties of ladies that ventured out beyond the barbed wire. I wanted to be a part of their group. The rations were always much better for the ladies in the working parties, too.

I convinced myself that Karin and Lasse would be okay just for one day, and explained to Karin how she could tell lies to get an extra ration for me, claiming I was sick in my bed.

From my private observation post behind some rocks, I overlooked the big square by the exit gate to the camp and saw the lorries and handcarts coming and going, mostly with foodstuffs and changing guards. Worst was the emptying of lorry-loads of cabbage and other greens directly onto the dusty, hard-baked ground next to the kitchens. It looked like pigswill, rotting and smelly. Just knowing that the food was for us made me feel sick. Even the rice was not fit for human consumption: it was full of maggots and mouse droppings. The bags were usually ripped, and the rice was just shovelled onto the ground. Two ladies were ordered to do the job.

During the early mornings I had observed the ladies who lined up for that day's departure to the fields beyond. As always, my curiosity got the better of me, and I could not help studying them. They wore straw hats and some had home-made 'sandals' made of cardboard, fastened and tied around their ankles and soles with fabric strips. They were a welcome item for the long, arduous day ahead, but most of the ladies were barefoot. They wore ragged cotton dresses or shorts, and carried picks and shovels. They had clearly been working out in the sun for too long: their skin was burned and wrinkled, with many red, open sores.

A party of guards marched out to meet the ladies and they bowed deeply. The guards counted them, yelled some instructions and then marched them out of the gate. I had heard a few of the women in our house talking and it was rumoured that the ladies on the outside working party got more food than we did and were even allowed a nap when the guards rested after lunch.

I desperately wanted to go and join them. I wanted more food and a nap and I wanted to see beyond the fence again, but the other ladies told me I was too small and the Japs would not allow it. I thought that if I found a large stone to stand on and then hid in between the women, perhaps I could trick the guards and make it out into the fields. The other three 'at home' could then get my ration.

Mama did not think this was a good idea and told me to forget it. But I would not give up that easily.

At six o'clock one morning I set out and stood in the square in shorts and a tattered shirt. I had even managed to borrow a straw hat to pull over my face. I did not manage to make any sandals, but that did not put me off. The ladies looked strangely at me and wondered what on earth I was doing there. 'I want to join you, if I may,' I said to them.

I stood on the stone I had found and thought I was both broad and tall enough to fool the guards, but when they arrived they just laughed and chased me away.

It took me three attempts before I succeeded and some of the ladies were very surprised. I was told in no uncertain terms to work at least as hard as them, otherwise the whole party would be punished. We stood in the darkness, waiting to leave. It was freezing cold and we all began to shiver. At one point we waited so long I was worried that maybe I had been noticed and they would turn me away again. As it turned out, we had to wait for the cart with the dead. I did not realize at the time, but the dead cart procession was a daily event. There were half a dozen bodies covered loosely with a sheet, but some arms and legs were visible. One of the nurses who cared for Mama when she was in the hospital pushed the cart and an armed guard walked alongside her. Some of the ladies bowed their heads when the cart passed us, but most hardly gave it a second glance; clearly it was something they were more than used to.

When the cart had disappeared out of sight, we were ordered towards the open gate and a handful of well-armed guards joined us. It was a strange feeling that came over me when the gates slammed shut behind us. At last I was out of that terrible camp and I felt a smile spread across my face as I tilted the straw hat even further to cover my joy. It had been so long since we had arrived at the camp and, as I walked away from it, I recalled how big everything seemed and how quiet it all was. The guards' rhythmic marching on the dusty road was the only thing that disturbed the silence.

We passed a few small villages, which were teeming with poultry, pigs and naked children. Then we were in a small town, with shops and bustling crowds. I lifted my hat and took everything in, for I had not seen anything like this for a long time. I really enjoyed it with all my senses. I wanted to linger and stare, but the guards were impatient and at one point made us run through the more densely populated areas. They did not like the way the natives stared at us. I, too, noticed the strangest looks on their faces: unfriendly, even hostile and angry.

At the end of a long road we turned off and took a path that led us to a huge plantation that was being run by the Japanese. One of the ladies whispered that the plantation had once belonged to a very important Dutch family, but they had been thrown into concentration camps. I hardly took in what the lady was saying; I was so amazed by what I was looking at. It was like entering a Garden of Eden, with shady trees, an abundance of tropical plants and the biggest display of flowers I had ever seen in every colour imaginable. My eyes took in everything; I had almost forgotten we had come to work. The Japanese quickly reminded us. We were gathered into an open space, and the shout went up: '*Tenko, tenko.*'

Beyond the square was a large bamboo shed, which would serve as the kitchen, and my stomach began to tell me how hungry I was. I had not eaten since the day before, and I hoped that maybe we would get something to eat and drink, a little breakfast, something different to help us with our work effort. But no, we were ordered into groups of three and four and made to march out into a big field several hundred metres away. Here we began to dig, sow, clean, rake and harvest for what turned out to be many hours. We tended to the tropical plants, roots and vegetables, cleaned the soil and pulled out weeds and small stones. The work was relentless and it seemed ridiculous to expect these emaciated, sick women to work so long and so hard in the full heat of the sun. But they did. I was told to fill a large bamboo basket with dirt and rubbish and empty it into a big hole where it would later be burned. The guards rested under the trees and watched us carefully. I made myself very visible so they would clearly be aware that, although I was small, I was still capable of work.

As the sun intensified and the Japs still didn't allow us any water, I began to regret my decision to join them. I started to take small rests when I thought no one was looking as I was getting dizzy and nauseous. The heat was now at its hottest and several of the women fainted. The Japs just laughed as they fell into the soil and watched as the other ladies carried them away. Finally, a signal was given and we were allowed to walk back to a shady place and sit down under the trees. We were given a tin cup with porridge and a bottle of water to drink. I had expected so much more. I had a good view across the fields from where I was sitting and noticed there were many other groups of 'workers' in the distance. When I asked one of the ladies where they had come from, she explained that they were men and young boys from another camp. When I looked hard I could just about tell the difference between the men and the boys. The lady said that they would be shot immediately if they got in touch with a female group.

Later in the afternoon, some women in our group tried to get close to the men's groups by chopping and weeding ever nearer to them. Most had husbands, brothers and even young sons in these dreaded camps and wanted to find out about them. It never worked: the Japs always stepped in just as it seemed a conversation would be possible with these poor, yellow, skeletal men. They would move the ladies to another section of the field and onto a different task. By now the heat was unbearable; the straw hats gave little or no protection from the sun as it was right over our heads. The skin on our arms and legs began to turn red and flabby. Some of the ladies had to sit down, and those with no hats were temporarily blinded and could hardly see the flowers and plants in front of them. At times I wondered if I could stand it any longer. The heat and thirst were so intense that eventually my legs gave way and finally I fell down face first into the soil. I lay there for a moment and it was the most comfortable place in the world. I did not want to get up; I had no energy left to move my legs and my back thanked me mercifully for the little respite. I was sure it would never repair itself, and nor would the deep red mark where the basket rested on my hip bone.

Try as I might, I could not get up again. One of the ladies called over to one of the guards and asked to get a cup of water. Thankfully he gave her permission. I managed to make it through to lunch and it was heaven just to lie down under the trees. The food consisted of two cups of rice mixed with cabbage soup. They allowed us an additional cup of water as well and, joy of all joys, a banana each. It was truly a great treat as I couldn't remember when I had enjoyed a whole banana to myself.

The break was over all too soon and how we managed to make it through until six in the evening is a mystery to me. The water we had enjoyed at lunch was the last we would see until we made it back to camp. Never had I felt so tired, so hot or so thirsty, and yet I dared not ease off for fear of the other women being punished. I carried my basket back and forth as the sweat poured from my body. Fortunately, towards the end of the day it had become a little cooler as the sun gradually lost its power. That was probably what helped us to make it back to the camp. I walked back along the same roads and through the same towns and villages, though I saw nothing. It was as if I was walking through a fog; I just wanted to be back at the camp and put my head under the water tap. The guards were tired, too, and obviously wanted to get back as soon as possible as they drove us on with their terrible bayonets, threatening us to move quickly. '*Leka*,' they yelled over and over again.

'The first day is the worst,' one of the ladies said. 'Then you get used to it.' She laughed. 'Either that or you die.'

I looked up into her eyes and could see she was not joking.

Back in the camp, my ordeal was not yet over. They made us take the customary *tenko*, counted us all several times and inspected the tools before we were allowed back to our houses. I dragged myself over to the house and my family and fell onto the blue door, totally exhausted, while the tears flowed. Mama, who was back from hospital, had been lying on her mattress inside, together with Lasse and Karin, but dragged herself out as she heard my sobbing. She brought me several cups of water and said she had been so afraid for me. I gasped through the tears that it was something I had wanted to try for a long time, but it was an experience I never wanted to repeat.

I never turned up on the parade for the work party again.

I was totally dehydrated and it took me several days to recover from the terrible ordeal. I'm convinced that I was closer to death then than at any other time in the camps.

CHAPTER 27

Young Boys, Old Men

It was a peculiar sight, a sight I was not used to. On my way to my private observation post I spotted them in a newly fenced-off area of the compound. As always, my curiosity got the better of me and I could not help walking over and standing with my nose to the fence.

I was looking at old men, skeletons of old men, lots of them, perhaps fifty or sixty. Some walked around the perimeter of the fence and talked with each other, but most sat in the shade of the barracks on the far side. I stood in shock. I could not believe how awful they looked. Most were dressed in nothing more than a pair of oversized baggy shorts tied up with string. They were dusty; all of them were barefoot, filthy, shaven-headed, starving, walking, talking corpses.

I called over to one of them, 'What are you doing here? Where are you going?' I was nervous as Mama had told me to stay away from any strangers that passed through the camp as they were likely to be carrying diseases.

A man shuffled over. I looked down at his legs, which were covered in huge ulcers and open wounds. His thighs were about the same width as his ankles and his torn, filthy shorts could not be done up properly because his stomach was so swollen with beriberi. His mouth was almost a black void, most of his teeth were missing and the remainder looked like an abandoned graveyard, and yet still he smiled.

'Who are you?' he asked.

'I am Lise,' I replied. 'I am Norwegian. What are you doing at Lampersarie?'

He looked around at the Japanese guards, obviously very wary of them, then he answered.

'Lampersarie . . . so that's where we are. The Nips tell us nothing at all. We are on our way to our next workplace, wherever that is.' He smiled again. 'Hopefully we might even get a little food. My name is Fred.'

He went on to explain that he was working on a railway where men died every hour. He said he would spare me the details, whatever that meant, but they were being moved and had to spend the night at Lampersarie.

'There are no trucks any more. We walk everywhere. Those that cannot walk are shot on the spot. But fear not, little treasure, the Allies are winning the war and I might be lucky enough to see my wife and little girl again soon.'

'The Allies are winning the war?' I questioned.

'Shhhh,' he said, looking round at the guards once again. 'It is true: the Australian truck drivers told us the bloody Nips are getting overrun everywhere, but they are so stubborn they won't surrender.'

This revelation left me speechless, and yet I found myself wondering if I could believe what the old man was saying. I had known him barely a minute. Should I tell Karin? Should I tell Mama and Lasse? Would it give them real hope or false hope? My head was full and I didn't know what to say. My new friend interrupted my thoughts.

'Do you know of a Dutch lady called Carla Buyse and a little girl called Yvonne? They were taken prisoner nearly three years ago. Have you heard of them? Are they alive? My little girl will be a little younger than you, perhaps seven or eight years old.' His eyes were sparkling now as the memories of his wife and child filled his head. I wanted so much to tell him they were in this camp and that they were safe and well, but I had never heard of any people by those names.

'I am sorry, no. I cannot recall a Carla or a little girl called Yvonne.'

The sparkle in his eyes seemed to die and his thin lips sagged as he hung his head. I tried to reassure him and return a little of the hope he had given me.

'This is a big camp, sir. There are thousands of people here and lots of little girls whose names I do not know.'

He nodded his head and turned slowly to walk away. He had taken a step or two when a puzzling thought came into my head.

'Fred,' I whispered after him.

He turned around. 'Yes?'

'How old are you?'

He thought for a second or two and his lips moved slowly, as if counting the years he'd been in captivity, then he looked me in the eye. ' . . . I am twenty-nine years old, Lise.'

It was the mothers' screaming that woke me. Karin and Lasse were both still sleeping and, as I crept outside to follow the noises, I could not have dreamed of the brutality I was about to witness; it was the worst I had seen in any of the camps so far and caused nightmares that would stay with me forever. I walked quickly, I don't know why. Karin and Lasse were safe with Mama. I thought about my friends in the house and Pieter, who for some reason I hadn't seen for some time. Mama had told me that Pieter was quite safe and that he hadn't disappeared like many of the others. Mama said that his mother was scared that they might send him away to the men's camps to work. The news coming from the men's camps was not good; there were stories of cruelty and many deaths and the work assigned to the starving men was extremely hard, with long, long hours and little food. I hurried now as I recognized a different scream, a boy's scream . . . Pieter, perhaps?

As I turned the corner at the end of the street, I could see the commotion in the distance, near to the entrance of the camp. I started to run as I heard another boy scream and, although my legs ached and stones bit into the soles of my feet, I kept on running.

I wish I hadn't.

I slowed to a walk, then a shuffle as the full horror of what I was witnessing became apparent. My eyes scanned the mothers, who were begging and pleading with the Japanese guards, and I now understood exactly what was happening.

Boys – not men, boys. The Japs were literally tearing them from their mothers' arms. They were sending them to the men's camps to work. To work and to die, if the rumours were right. One of the mothers lay on the ground unconscious, blood pouring from a gaping head wound, and her son was trying in vain to cling onto her while two Japanese guards pulled him from her. He was crying, shouting out, 'Mami . . . Mami . . .'

He was no more than ten years of age, not a man, a boy . . . a child. One of the Japs took him by the hair and dragged him from the still body of his mother. He pulled him across the dusty ground and kicked out at him, ordering him to take *tenko*. The poor child did as he was told, all the time looking over at the prone figure of his mother, who was now showing signs of movement. Other boys were pulled, pushed and kicked towards him and, in a short while, a line of six boys stood shoulder to shoulder, bowing in the direction of the Japanese soldiers. The mothers had resigned themselves to the inevitability of the situation. They were all aware, as we all were, that resisting our captors meant certain death.

The mothers huddled together with younger brothers, sisters and friends. They wept openly and hugged each other; some offered a token wave to the boys. The oldest boy would be aged about twelve, the youngest being the ten-year-old, who still watched the stirring body of his mother.

A Japanese officer walked over and the guards stood stiffly to attention; the boys stood with their heads bowed. The officer did not appear to be very happy as he ordered the boys to stand up straight, then he quickly walked up the line. He was shouting something at them in Japanese and the boys did not seem to understand. He looked over at the group, including their mothers, and a couple of the ladies walked forward and handed something to the officer. I strained to see what it was and became aware of some of the mothers running back to their houses. The Japanese officer stood, growing redder and angrier by the minute.

One by one the ladies returned and they all held something in their hands. I could now see what it was they were holding: they had the boys' cardboard numbers.

The officer turned his back on the mothers and addressed the boys. He spoke in English, announcing that the small boys were now men and that they were very privileged that they could now serve the glorious Japanese Emperor. He waved the numbers in front of them and read them out one by one. The boys were ordered to come out of the line and collect their individual numbers.

He spoke. 'Numbers worn at all times.'

He turned and walked slowly towards their mothers. I barely heard him telling them to return to their houses and prepare for the boys to leave. The mothers sobbed as they trudged off, and several minutes later they all returned. The boys all had a bottle of water and one of the smaller boys even had some sandals, but he was the only one. Two of the boys had some spare items of clothing, but the bigger children had nothing. They had grown out of their shirts and stood there in nothing more than a pair of dirty, ragged shorts.

The Japanese officer seemed to be a little happier now; he was even smiling. He ordered the boys to dress and those that had shirts put them on. The little boy with the shoes put them on quickly. The gates opened and a lorry trundled in. As it pulled up in front of the line and turned around to face the gates again, I noticed other young boys in the back looking very scared; they were all very quiet.

The boys in line waited for a command from the officer.

He stepped forward and spoke to one of the older boys. 'Numbers to be worn on chests at all times.'

He asked the boy where his shirt was and the boy shook his head. The officer took a step forward and took the cardboard number from the boy.

No, I thought . . . surely not . . . he's a child.

But he did.

He nodded at two of the guards, who took their positions on either side of the frightened boy. They held one arm each.

The Japanese officer opened up the safety pin and gathered the loose skin of the boy's chest between his thumb and forefinger. And while the boy struggled and screamed, the officer forced the rusty pin through the flesh and snapped the clasp shut. The blood poured from the boy's chest as several of the women who had huddled together fainted. The officer turned towards them and repeated his statement.

'Numbers worn at all times.'

He turned to the next bare-chested boy, who made a vain attempt to run, realizing he was next in line. A guard tripped him as he tried to run past and pounced on him before he could get to his feet. The poor boy struggled with all the strength he had left in him, but it was no good, and eventually the blood ran down his chest, too, the safety pin firmly in place, the weight of the piece of cardboard pulling at his skin. I watched, unable to comprehend what I was seeing. The tears rolled down his cheeks as he looked over to his mother. I could see what he was thinking and I was thinking exactly the same thing. Why don't you help me? Why do they do what they do? If the Japanese could be this cruel to children in front of their mothers, what would it be like at the men's camp?

I watched, numb with shock and fighting my tears, as the boys were herded like goats onto the back of the lorry. The mothers had come forward now, eager for a last touch, a last kiss from their sons, but more Japs stood at the back of the lorry with their bayonets pointed at the women. The officer gave a signal to the driver and he crunched it into gear and started to move off. The poor boys hanging out of the back of the lorry, pleading with their mamas to rescue them, is an image that will never leave me. Apparently they were on their way to Bangkong Camp, where we had come from.

CHAPTER 28

Finding and Losing Oma

❧❧❧

It was a truly special moment; wonderful news: Papa was alive.

Mama had been pushed from the hospital once again on the handcart and, as she called from afar, I could see her smiling, and the two ladies pushing her were smiling, too. By the time she delivered her news, Lasse and Karin were smiling and I nearly cried tears of happiness.

Mama waved something in her hand. 'He is alive,' she shouted. 'Papa is alive. We will ask the ladies to help us with the translation,' she said. We knew some Bahasa Malay, but it was important to us to get it right.

She handed the postcard to me.

Sure enough, as I studied the postcard, I recognized Papa's handwriting, even though I hadn't seen it for so very long. The message was brief, simple and to the point, but his words meant so much to us:

Dear Kirsten,
I hope you are well and safe, how is it with the children? Are
they okay? Do you have enough money? I hope this war will
soon be over so we can all come home. I hope Lise, Karin and
Lasse are fine.

I have not heard from you, look after yourself and keep well
until we meet again.

All my love,
Dan

There was Japanese writing on the other side of the postcard,
which we couldn't understand, and the card didn't say where he
was, but it did not matter. We were all elated and, as Mama was
helped from the cart, we hugged and kissed each other. I could
hear other families celebrating, too. Why had the Japs suddenly
allowed a postcard after all these years? Had Fred been telling
the truth after all? Were the Japs suddenly turning nice because
they knew they were losing the war?

Mama reached into her pocket and brought out a blank piece
of card. 'And we can even write back to him,' she announced
with a smile.

The atmosphere in the camp had definitely changed; it felt
more relaxed and I began to notice that the Japanese guards who
had patrolled the camp for so long now spent most of the time in
their barrack huts playing cards. I noticed also their expressionless
faces, and that they didn't appear to be so angry and superior. The
tenkos, too, had all but disappeared. The only thing that hadn't

changed was the awful food, the lack of it and the absence of medicine in the hospital. Mama was back in hospital again, so there was nobody to control me or curb my daring, and I was constantly on the search for food. I recall taking even more risks than before.

I was walking past the stairs leading up to the Japanese commandant's office. It was a place where I always felt nervous, because just on the other side of the fence was the place where the poor lady had a pistol held to her head when we first arrived at the camp. It was the grains of rice on the steps that gave me the courage. I figured that grains of rice on the stairs meant the commandant's office was where the officers' rice was stored, and I knew that the commandant always left his office for breakfast at about nine o'clock each day.

The next day I returned. I stood for several minutes, watching for the commandant to leave and, sure enough, before long I saw him walk through the main gate.

It was time to put my plan into action. I had even managed to collect some wood to cook the rice and I had a secret place where I could start a fire so that no one would see me.

I stood at the bottom of the steps and looked around. There wasn't a guard in sight and I smiled; this was going to be easy.

I knelt down on the first step, picked up two or three grains of rice and put them into my pocket. As I climbed each step, the grains of rice increased and I carefully collected every single bit, taking care to look behind me as I got nearer to my prize. I was three steps from the top now but, to my disappointment, I could hear Japanese voices. They were coming from the commandant's office and I realized that some of the guards were inside. Of course, how stupid of me; they were there to protect the rations.

I wasn't going to give up, though. I would take a peek in the commandant's office to see how close the sacks were to the door. As I reached the level of the top step, I pushed myself onto my stomach and slithered towards the office like a snake. My heart was pounding and I could hardly breathe for the fear inside my body.

I could now see the Japs on the other side of the desk. They were smoking and playing cards and were not looking in my direction. I turned my head to the sacks by the door and wondered why the Japs could not hear my heartbeat, as it was louder than any noise in the room. I knew I had to make a decision soon. The decision was easy. Even now, with a mere handful of rice in my pocket, I would be labelled a thief if I was caught. I would be shot and Mama would be punished, too. It simply wasn't worth the risk and at least I had a little extra rice that I had collected from the stairs. I hadn't been caught and all I needed to do was slide slowly back away from the office, climb down the stairs and run away.

But when I noticed that one of the sacks was split and the rice had spilled out onto the floor, the pull was too great. With one eye on the sacks and one eye on the guards, I dragged myself across the cool tiled floor. I grimaced as a tiny shard of cracked ceramic tile pierced the skin on my knee and part of me wanted to back out and run. But I was only a metre from the sack now; I was past the point of no return and all I could think of was the full bellies of Karin, Lasse and me later that day. I wondered what a full belly felt like; it had been so long.

I reached the sack and pushed my hand inside. The sack tore and I screwed my eyes tightly shut as the noise reverberated around the room, convinced it would be heard. I waited for a noise, footsteps or a shout from the guards, but I heard nothing. I opened my eyes again and looked across the room. The guards were still playing, smoking and laughing and they had not spotted me.

I pulled out a huge handful and pushed it into my pocket, then another, which I placed in the other pocket. I had achieved my mission – two huge pocketfuls of first-class rice – and I almost broke into a smile. I did not dare to turn around; instead I slithered out backwards very slowly. I dared not make a noise or a sudden movement and eventually I made it to the steps. I stood up and was so elated that a smile came as I patted the contents of my pockets.

I was halfway down the stairs when a soft voice stopped me in my tracks and I froze in horror.

'You . . . little girl . . . stop!'

But it was not a Japanese growl; it was European and female and it was very familiar to me.

'Lise . . . is that you?'

I looked to my right and, sitting on the low balustrade of the steps, was a lady who looked and sounded like . . . Oma, the Governor's wife I called Grandma back in Surabaya.

'What have you been doing up there?' she asked.

It was such a shock. I thought I was staring at a ghost. Surely it wasn't Oma; she looked awful . . . nothing like the image I had in my head. She had always been a plump, well-built lady back then and, as I recalled, she was very strict and correct and smelled of lavender. Her hair was always neat and pretty and she dressed well.

I walked over to the skin and bones of the lady dressed in rags and she took my hands.

'Where have you been, Lise?'

The words would hardly come out of my mouth, such was my shock at the sight of the woman who sat in front of me on the concrete balustrade. Her legs were swollen like Mama's and her face and thin body were a mass of open, infected sores. I wondered why she was not in the hospital. She prompted me again.

'Well?'

I opened my pockets and proudly showed her the rice. I said I'd stolen it from under the noses of the Nips.

She scolded me, shook me by the arm and made me promise that I would never do it again.

I asked where Opa was, the man I had called Grandad, her husband. She sat up straight, her eyes moistened and her bottom lip began to tremble.

'I don't know where Opa is . . . I think he is dead. Opa is probably dead and Miep, too.'

Miep was her daughter.

'We were all taken at the same time and separated immediately. I have searched this camp for months, but Miep is not here.'

She looked straight through me into space. 'I hope they are dead.' Then the tears started. 'I hope they have not gone through what I have gone through. Death is surely better.' She sobbed and then composed herself. 'How is your family, Lise?'

I told her all about Mama and Karin and Lasse and the postcard we had received from Papa. I thought my news would raise a little smile on Oma's face, but it was not to be.

'Go quickly, Lise, get rid of your rice. I will see you tomorrow.'

Oma gave me a quick cuddle and I walked as fast as I could back to the blue door.

It was the last time I saw her.

Several days later I went looking for her again, but I never found her.

My immediate concern was how to cook the rice as I had to find something to cook it in. I found an old tin near the rubbish bins and felt very pleased with myself as I washed it clean. I now had everything I needed to cook the rice. I filled the tin with water, took it outside and placed it by the toilet door. Then I ran back into our room and collected some matches and paper. My plan was to cook the rice in the outside toilet; it was a place that people only went near if they had to and, of course, the Nips had their own toilets, so they never ventured by. I had a big piece of card and, as I started the fire, I began wafting the smoke away. The sticks of wood I had found were bone-dry and once the fire took hold there was very little smoke, so I knew I would be safe.

I placed the tin on the burning wood and watched as it quickly came to the boil. I held my nose and closed my eyes as I lay back against the wall and rested. The whole exercise had taken a lot out of me and I fought the urge to sleep.

But something was wrong.

The fire was still burning well and glowing red underneath and yet the place suddenly filled with smoke. I heard someone shouting in Dutch and moving the door away. 'Put that fire out . . . put that fire out.'

I ignored her and pulled the tin from the fire. The water was gone and I looked in the dust at a big wet patch oozing from the fire, sizzling as it flowed like a small river. No, no . . . the tin had a leak. I found a tiny hole on the seam where it had been welded.

The rice on the bottom was black, but I mixed it all together with my spoon. It looked fine; it hadn't boiled for long, but I was sure it would be okay.

Karin and I forced ourselves to chew on the hard grains of rice; we were so hungry and excited at our extra rations. Lasse took two or three grains and spat them out onto the ground. While we ate I relayed the story about my mission inside the Japanese commandant's office and how I had met Oma on the steps. We finished every single grain and, yes, our stomachs felt full for the first time in a long while as we sat back and patted them, satisfaction written across our faces. Karin and I wished we had followed Lasse's lead when, during the early hours of the next morning, our stomachs swelled and felt as if they would explode. We were ill for nearly two days and I gave up any more thoughts about stealing uncooked rice again.

CHAPTER 29

Rumours Abound

~~~~

After Mama had been back from hospital for a couple of days Mrs Antje had looked in on her and made her stand up. She just about managed it but, when Mrs Antje persuaded her to take a few steps, it was clear Mama was in great pain, despite her protests. Mrs Antje and a friend returned some time later with the handcart and Mama was taken away to hospital again.

By this time I had joined Bible lessons, which were given by Jolien. The classes were taken on the blue door with Lasse, Karin and me, and generally a couple of others who had to sit on the ground. Sometimes Pieter even ventured onto the door in his dress. By now his hair was very long, and if a stranger or a guard wandered by, he simply looked down so that his hair covered his face. Jolien told the most wonderful, beautiful stories about God, the Bible and Jesus and his disciples. She told us about miracles and parables, how Jesus turned water into wine, how he made crippled men walk and how he fed five thousand people with just three loaves of bread and five fishes. She told each story with a passion and a real belief in what she was talking about.

To me, it didn't make any sense.

I had talked with Mama some weeks earlier and asked her about God. She told me she had lost her faith and God could simply not exist; if He did, He was no better than these evil Japs whom He allowed to keep women and children prisoner, torturing and murdering them.

She said she couldn't pray to God any more. 'God has done nothing about these evil men,' she ranted. 'Don't mention God to me. Everyone's morals have gone. Even in the camp among the prisoners there is no solidarity; different nationalities are fighting each other like animals.'

I confess Mama made more sense than Jolien.

But still I went to the blue door when Bible lessons were held. Jolien said it was important to hear about nice things in order to keep our spirits up. I guess I went there out of boredom more than anything else and, of course, to see the faces of the children, which for once were happy. I enjoyed watching them as Jolien spoke.

But there was another reason I listened in on Jolien's lessons.

Jolien had heard rumours about the Americans beating the Japanese in Asia, and that the war in Europe had ended with victory for our Allies. She told us that the Japanese were ready to surrender.

I wanted to believe Jolien so much, I really did, but could I believe everything she was saying or was it just another made-up story, like the ones in her Bible?

When I visited Mama in the hospital I told her Jolien's story about the Americans and Mama grinned and said she had heard the nurses talking about it, too. Mama said hundreds of thousands of Japanese had been killed and the war was coming to an end. She said that some of the nurses had demanded more medicines and food from the Japs and, for once, they had complied with their wishes. For the first time we had eggs and other things to cook, and the Japanese guards were nowhere to be seen.

Every day now we could see United States aeroplanes flying overhead. The Japanese would sound the siren, the same siren as for *tenko*, then they would run for cover, disappearing into their barracks or bunkers. We just stood and watched the planes flying high in the sky, somehow understanding that there would be little point wasting bombs on such a tragic place as Camp Lampersarie.

The following day, Jolien told us that God had arranged the victory for the Allies, but then she said four thousand people had died in the camp at Lampersarie and many more would not make it out alive. Again, that didn't make any sense to me. When I questioned her, she said that God had been testing our faith, but surely he could have set an easier task?

Jolien said we must be on our guard against the Japs and the Indonesians outside, as everyone was very worried and tense. She said we could all be home in a matter of a few months, but that we must not take any chances. We had to wait and see in which direction God pointed us. She said He would look after us, but that we must be patient.

It was true: the Japs did not bother us any more and some-times even left the gate to the camp unguarded. There were other rumours coming from outside the camp now: that the Indonesians were attacking some of the prisoners who had tried to escape. Jolien said the Indonesians were angry with the people who had occupied their land for so long and wanted them to leave now that the war was coming to an end. She said that the Dutch had been on the island of Java for nearly three hundred years.

'Then I will be safe,' I said, 'I am Norwegian.'

Jolien shook her head. 'It matters not, Lise. You are European; to them you are the same . . . you are a blanc.'

Jolien was right. I had heard the expression 'blanc' many times. I had heard the native boys and girls shouting it at us from the other side of the fence.

'You are safer in the camp for the time being,' she said.

Now I was sad and angry. I wanted to shout at Jolien about her God. There were no bayonets any more and no more *tenkos*. The Japs were no longer hostile and yet, just as it looked as if we were safe from the Japs, a new enemy was gathering on the other side of the fence.

The extra food and medicine Mama was getting meant she was back with us and spending many hours on her blanket on the blue door. I noticed that she had learned to smile again.

Everyone outside was cheering. I didn't understand. Mama said the war was over; the Americans had dropped two of the biggest bombs ever known on the Japanese cities of Hiroshima and Nagasaki. Surely now the Japanese Emperor had to surrender.

I had been cooking some pancakes on a tin lid and was annoyed that people were disturbing me. The end of the war could wait. I was hungry and couldn't remember the last time I'd been allowed to cook on an open fire in full view of everyone.

Gradually it sank in. The war was over. I took the pancakes over to the blue door and sat with Mama, Lasse, Karin, Jolien and Mrs Antje. Mrs Antje and Jolien hugged each other. I had never seen Mama so happy. She was so happy she couldn't even eat my lovely burned pancakes, and she was so excited she got up and walked a few steps. I hadn't seen her walk for months. She took two or three steps, I remember it well, and then we helped her back onto the blue door as she took a series of deep breaths.

'We are safe now,' she said. 'The war is over,' she kept repeating again and again.

Strangers were walking freely into the camp and they were not challenged by the Japanese, who simply kept out of the way. There were some Dutch military men from the KNIL (Koninklijk Nederlandsch Indisch Leger, Royal Dutch East Indies Army) and men from the Red Cross. They warned us to stay in the camp for safety reasons and incredibly Mrs Antje told us that the Japs were now protecting us from the hostile natives outside. This was terrible and something I couldn't quite believe. I thought back to our home in Surabaya and my Javanese friends, the servants and the gardeners – they were always so nice and friendly. Why had they changed? Was this how war affected people?

CHAPTER 30

Escape from Camp Lampersarie

❧❧❧

Red Cross parcels started coming into the camp: small rations of chocolate, sugar, condensed milk, corned beef and sometimes biscuits. I remember vomiting on several occasions when I overloaded my stomach.

The gates were now open for a few hours every day and two Japanese guards stood with their rifles pointing out into the *kampong*. Several native adults and children stood several metres away with menacing looks on their faces. It was true: the Japs were protecting us. However, there were times that the gates were left unguarded and, when there were no native Javanese around, a few people ventured outside. When the Japs returned they were ordered back inside, but there were no harsh words, beatings or punishments; they just wandered back into the camp.

We still had money and were told we could buy fruit at the local market if we could get out, but not many people dared. It was still very unsafe and there were stories of Dutch people being beaten to death by Indonesians. Pieter and I discussed going outside and agreed with each other that children would be safe. He was now wearing shorts and a shirt, had short hair and loved it. We took a walk outside a few days later and thought it was a great adventure, even though the atmosphere in the village was a little unpleasant. We managed to buy a few bananas in the market and then returned quickly to camp.

Later that week a hand grenade was thrown into the camp, killing two ladies, and gangs of natives threw stones, bricks and sticks at anyone who ventured near the fence. I was terrified and at the same time very confused about the actions of the locals. Many people tried to get away from the camp, but the escapees were always attacked by the Javanese and disappeared.

There was better news when we returned to the blue door later that day. Mama explained that Uncle Axel and Aunt Marianne had arranged a safe escape from the camp. Mama emphasized that we couldn't tell anyone. A nurse had been contacted by the Swedish Red Cross people and Uncle Axel had paid one of the guards on the gate a lot of money to 'disappear' at the right moment.

Mama's health had improved dramatically and each day, with more food and medicine, she grew stronger as we waited for further instructions. One morning, when it was still dark, someone knocked on our door and told us to be at the exit gate in an hour. We gathered our possessions quietly and secretly so that no one would notice. Mama swallowed some painkillers so that she could walk all the way to the gate when necessary. She stood by the blue door wearing her pretty dress. It was still dark.

For Mama it was an enormous effort, but slowly but surely she made it, with Karin and me holding her up and almost carrying her each step of the way.

We sat next to the closed gate. It was very quiet and there was no one around, not even a Japanese guard. Mama said that the gate would be opened soon. We waited for nearly an hour and, as it got light, people started to wander through the camp. When two Japanese guards took up their positions on either side of the gate, Mama said we had to go back.

She cried all the way back to the house and we cried, too. Mama was so disappointed and severely exhausted, too, as her legs gave way just beside the blue door. People in the house were puzzled. Mama was wearing a dress. They asked a few questions but Mama didn't answer. They helped her back into the room and we lay down again; we were worn out.

It was early afternoon before I had the energy to go out and get some food. Mama never moved the whole day.

A few days later the same thing happened: we heard a whisper around six in the morning, telling us to be there by seven. We had to support Mama once again and we fed Lasse chocolate to keep him quiet.

This time the gates were ajar and, as we walked towards them, I noticed that there was only one Japanese guard there. As he saw us approaching, he turned his back to us and lit a cigarette.

We walked through the gates slowly and quietly. It was a strange sensation, not knowing if the guard would change his mind and start shooting at us for trying to escape.

The shots never came.

Mama said we had to look for a man with transport. It was early in the morning and there was no one to be seen. However, as we turned the corner, we spotted an Indonesian with a donkey and a dough cart. The man was fast asleep. We woke him and he helped us up onto the cart. He slapped at the donkey with a stick and we set off.

This was it; we were on our way to freedom. I should have been elated and excited, like Mama, Karin and Lasse, but I wasn't. I hadn't said goodbye to Pieter and my other friends, Jolien, Kitty, Mrs Antje and, of course, I hadn't seen Oma or Miep. I was feeling so very sorry that we hadn't even said goodbye and, as silly as it seemed, I was going to miss every single one of them. I hoped that they, too, would escape Camp Lampersarie soon.

Despite this a part of me didn't feel guilty, and I was ashamed of myself. The Japs had taught me many lessons during the period they brutalized and desensitized me in captivity. They had taught me to be selfish, not to feel guilt and to survive at the expense of others. I remembered the food I had pilfered from the kitchen area and the hospital, and the special rice from the commandant's office and, at that point in time, I realized that at least I had not taken the food from some other poor wretch's starving mouth.

The man with the donkey spoke little on the journey. He told us he had been paid to take us to a railway station, where we would be met by a Swiss man. The poor donkey looked starving, too; his ribs stuck out as he trotted along the dusty, hot road, and I whispered under my breath for him to go faster and put as much distance between us and the camp as possible. The further and longer we travelled, the more at ease I felt and yet, every now and again, Mama told us we must be careful; we were not out of danger. She told us not to laugh or run around when we got to the station, as the last thing we wanted was to draw attention to ourselves.

We were with the man and his donkey for about an hour. When he left us at the railway station at Semarang he said '*Selemat Jalan*' (have good travel). I remembered that expression from Surabaya. I had not heard it in nearly three years.

The station was like something I had never witnessed before, not even in the camps. It seemed as if everyone in the world wanted to travel and everyone in the world wanted to travel that day. There were Japanese guards at the station who didn't really seem interested in what was going on, and Javanese and Chinese people as well. Looking around carefully, I spotted quite a few Europeans. This made me feel a little better.

Mama looked very anxious. 'What is wrong, Mama?' I asked. She explained that we had to meet a Swiss man who had our tickets, but how was she supposed to find him in such a crowd, especially as she didn't know what he looked like? Mama was in a quandary: she needed to be seen so that the Swiss man could find us, and yet she didn't want to attract any attention either.

We were there for at least another hour, and all the time Mama grew more and more agitated. She stood in the queue for tickets and, when she got to the official, asked if any tickets had been left. The man shook his head and Mama returned to us crying. She was in pain once more as she had drunk the water containing her painkillers. Just then a man in a crumpled white suit approached us. He wore a floppy white hat, which was pulled down over his face, and he appeared very nervous. I recognized him: he was the nice friendly man that used to visit our house in Surabaya. As he put an envelope in Mama's hands, he looked frightened and said he could be shot for helping us. Then he was gone; no conversation, pleasant greetings or good-byes. But Mama didn't care. We had our tickets and would soon be on our way.

We pushed on to the platform where the train left for Surabaya. On the train I felt very conspicuous. We were the only white people in the whole carriage, even though it was very crowded. I was aware of lots of suspicious eyes looking at us. Mama managed to find a single seat and Lasse fell onto her lap while Karin and I sat at her feet. Mama opened the envelope and went ashen-grey. I asked her what was wrong. She became tearful again and explained that there was only one ticket in the envelope. She thought there would be more; this had to be a mistake. I shrugged my shoulders. 'What does that mean?' I asked. She explained that she had three children without tickets. Lasse would probably be okay to ride without a ticket, but Karin and I could be thrown off the train. Mama hatched a plan and said that if we spotted a ticket conductor we should disappear. She was happy again when the train started moving.

The train was so full that people even hung on the outside.

We were tired and thirsty and Karin and I lay in the aisle most of the way, keeping one eye open for the man who could throw us off the train. We had fruit and a little bread. It tasted good. There were no more bayonets, no nasty men shouting at us, but nevertheless, at each station, I feared it was only a matter of time before the Japanese guards would board the train and drag us back to Camp Lampersarie.

The further we went, the better I felt. Eventually I even fell asleep, curled up in a ball under one of the seats. We were on the train for nearly twelve hours and it was dark when we arrived at Surabaya.

We didn't know what to do when we got there, so we walked outside. 'It's nice to be back in Surabaya,' I said to Mama. She nodded and gave me a smile.

Then we heard someone shouting at us in Indonesian. He was calling, '*Datang, datang,*' (come, come). He walked over to us and took Mama's bag. '*Datang,*' he repeated and we walked behind him to a big black car as he opened the boot and threw everything in. Standing at the front of the car was Uncle Axel.

Uncle Axel, Mama and then Lasse, Karin and I all broke down sobbing. Everyone was so emotional and Uncle Axel was clearly shocked by our appearance. He said he wanted to hug us, but was frightened we would all break. He helped us into the car and lifted Mama's legs up onto a pillow, which was placed on the flap seat.

He told us we were now safe in the hands of the Swedish consul. Mama cried again, but I could see almost instantly how she relaxed as soon as the driver started the engine and pulled away.

We didn't know where to start telling the horrific story of our years in the camps at the hands of the Japanese. Aunt Marianne had given Uncle Axel some biscuits and water and he fed us during the journey, but Mama kept telling us to be careful as our stomachs would still need to adjust.

I sat in the beautiful clean car, looking at the lights of Surabaya, and thought, At last . . . it is all over.

CHAPTER 31

Emma Park, Surabaya

❧

When the gate to number 11 Emma Park closed behind us, it was a special, special moment. The reunion with Aunt Marianne was so emotional; she cried and cried and I recall, too, the shocked look on her face as she set eyes on our skinny little bodies. I had a feeling that we were safe, that no one could touch us, and that Uncle Axel would protect us forever. Two of the servants helped Mama upstairs and into the bath. The servants told her that Aunt Marianne had said that all her old clothes should be burned and new clothes had been laid out on the bed. Aunt Marianne had run a bath for Karin and me, and we got in together. She poured a smelly liquid into the bath and, as we pushed the water around, it filled with bubbles. The soap stung our open scars and sores, but it didn't matter because I knew it was cleaning them. It was almost a nice sting, a nice pain. It was simply magical, and when I got out, Aunt Marianne dried me with a huge white fluffy towel and told me that she'd given

Mama perfume and a nice dress and that within the next hour we would all be sitting down to a big feast. There were beautiful soft sheets on my bed and pillows and curtains to pull to keep out the night, but, best of all, there were no scorpions or cockroaches, no rats or mice, and definitely no Nips anywhere to be seen.

I really looked forward to sleeping in a bed. Everything was perfect, but now I was hungry.

The table was set in the dining room and there were some other people sitting around it: two Swedish friends of Uncle Axel and three Danish escapees who had been there a few days. They looked altogether fatter and better than us and I asked which camp they had been in as they had clearly been better fed than we had. They laughed and one of them explained that they, too, had been starved and tortured by the Japs and that it was only the last few days feasting on Aunt Marianne's biscuits that had made them fatter.

We sat quietly at the table and I looked in amazement at the shining knives, forks and spoons, at the candles and crisp white serviettes. An Indonesian man wearing a white suit and a colourful turban appeared with some hot plates, but they were empty. I started crying harder than I had ever cried in any of the camps, and Uncle Axel asked me what was wrong. Between the tears I sobbed that Aunt Marianne had promised me more food than I could dream of, and here we were with empty plates.

The food came soon after: potatoes, soup, meat and

Indonesian-style fish, bread and cheeses, rice and a big bowl of stew.

A servant asked me what I wanted.

'Just rice,' I said.

'Just rice?' she said with a puzzled look on her face.

'Just rice,' I said. 'No bugs or spiders, no worms or dirt, just fluffy white rice.'

A little later I had some soup, too, and then finished with ice cream and fruit. I think Aunt Marianne was a little disappointed that I didn't try anything else as she had said we could have anything we wanted. I couldn't explain why I didn't want anything else to eat and, although everything looked and smelled nice, I had forgotten what other food was like. I watched the Indonesian, scared that he would take the food away, and I almost hugged my plate until it broke. I was conscious of the others looking at me, but they were not going to steal my fluffy white rice. For a moment I wondered if I should discreetly stuff some rice in my pockets, just in case . . .

We went up to bed as soon as the meal was finished. I slept with Karin in a huge double bed with a canopy and we convinced ourselves that it wasn't a dream. I kept smelling the sheets and the pillows, soft flowery smells, everything clean, and it seemed to take forever to fall asleep.

It wasn't a dream after all. Karin and I woke up at the same time and grinned at each other; as if by magic we knew what the other was thinking.

Breakfast was laid at the same table and it was another feast.

I'm sure there was everything on that table I could ever remember eating for breakfast at one time or another. There were small slices of bacon, sausages, porridge, eggs, cereal and cakes. The bread was soft and fresh and warm, not a bit of green mould anywhere to be seen. This time I knew it wasn't a dream, and this time I had no option but to try the other food as there was no rice. Mama told me all the time to be careful and to eat small portions. I did as she said, but I still felt sick when I left the table.

Soon afterwards a doctor checked us over and applied cream and bandages to our sores. Then he went to see Mama, who had taken to her bed after breakfast. He was with her a long time and she remained in her bed for the rest of the day. Aunt Marianne took her supper in on a tray.

Mama looked a lot better after a couple of days. I went into her room and she was sitting in a nice chair with her feet up, looking so very happy. After the two feasts we felt a little unwell and for many days Uncle Axel and Aunt Marianne arranged just small, light meals. Our bandages were changed daily and Lasse slept almost permanently, as did Karin. Aunt Marianne explained that it was part of the recovery process. Many days passed.

One day I asked to go outside and reluctantly Mama allowed us out with one of the servants. She explained that war had broken out on Java and it was dangerous to be out on our own. We didn't care; we were having a great time. I was on a borrowed bicycle, riding with the servant while Karin and Lasse ran behind us. Then we heard shooting and the servant panicked and started shouting at us to take cover. I dropped the bicycle and ran for Lasse, and then we all ran back to the gate as fast as our legs would carry us. Lasse complained that his stomach was hurting as he bounced up and down on my hip when I ran. I heard more gunfire that seemed close by, and I wasn't going to stop no matter how hard he cried.

The Indonesians lay on the rooftops shooting at the whites, the servant explained to Uncle Axel, and he was furious, saying that their anger should be directed at the Japanese. I heard Uncle Axel on the telephone to someone later in the day; he told them that an internal war had broken out on Java and they were even shooting at children. He told the person on the phone that he would need to get us all back to Europe.

The next day, as I carried a tray of food into the lounge, a filthy, tall, skinny man stood in front of me, wearing a vest hanging over a huge pair of shorts held up with some string. His skin was yellowish, like parchment, and there was no life to it. He looked sick and so very thin. It was Papa.

I never found out where Papa had been held or how he had been treated as he refused to talk about it. He simply told me he had escaped with a couple of friends and that was that. He was terrified those first few days that the Japs would come calling on Uncle Axel and take him back to the camp. I watched him taking his first bath and remembered how good it had felt when I had had my first bath in nearly three years. As Papa climbed from the bath, I noticed at least a dozen angry red scars on his back. I asked how he got them, but he never answered.

In the coming weeks, Uncle Axel and Aunt Marianne prepared to vacate the Swedish consulate, where they had lived for
nearly twenty years. Uncle Axel seemed to be on the telephone
permanently, making arrangements to leave.

Finally transport came. I was terrified as it was the same type
of open-backed truck we had been taken away in. I hated them
and told anyone who would listen that I wouldn't get in. Mama
put her arms around me and persuaded me that it was far more
dangerous to stay in Surabaya; she told me we were going home
to Norway and suddenly my head was filled with images of snow
and fjords, the smiling faces of Grandma and Grandad, my
cousins, and walks in the park with thick coats, woolly hats and
gloves. Was it really happening? Were we going home?

The truck was full and Mama said we were going to the port
and onto a ferry to Singapore. There were five trucks going down
to the harbour, all driving in a line together, and each truck
had seats and at least two men carrying guns. Uncle Axel led
the way, driving in front in the consulate car. About twenty
minutes into the journey there was a terrible explosion in front
of us. Some of the men jumped out and we were ordered into the
forest to hide while they inspected the trucks. One of the men
explained that a bomb had been fastened under the third truck
and had blown it up.

'Many people are dead,' he explained.

Very quickly the rest of the trucks were inspected, then we
were loaded back on and set off again. As we passed the truck
that had blown up, it was still on fire and a mass of twisted burn-

ing metal. Many bloody bodies lay on the side of the road and I cried out for someone to help them.

'No one can help them, my dear,' one of the gunmen said. 'They are dead.'

'But we can't just leave their bodies,' I said tearfully.

'We can,' he said, 'and we must. It's about survival; we have to get out of here. It's very dangerous.'

I looked out of the back of the truck as gradually the bodies disappeared from sight. Everyone was quiet, in shock, thinking about what had happened as the remaining trucks trundled on. My mind was full of the horrible end these poor people had experienced after years of starvation and deprivation. They had been so looking forward to a wonderful new life, only to be blown up and killed in this awful way.

Eventually we arrived at the docks and the convoy of trucks stopped. Uncle Axel pointed at a huge car ferry and smiled. 'That's our ship,' he said. 'It's going to take us to Singapore.'

CHAPTER 32

En Route Home

❧❧

I don't remember the name of the ship that took us to Singapore. I just remember that it was very big and we only set sail after Uncle Axel had sorted out the paperwork and money. I remember we had lots of good food and we were very well looked after.

When we arrived in Singapore we were taken to a huge Red Cross tent and given clothes. Karin and I were given skirts, blouses, pyjamas, underwear, woollen socks and some thick brown leather shoes. The shoes were so uncomfortable. I had not worn shoes for over two years and, although at first they were a bit of a novelty, after a dozen steps or so wearing horrible woollen socks they were like wearing blocks of cement. I recall saying to Mama that I would never get used to shoes like that. She smiled. 'Oh yes, you will,' she said, 'especially when we get to Norway and we encounter the snow and ice.' I was also given a pair of tennis shoes, which I changed into immediately. We spent three days in a nice hotel in Singapore, but I remember being annoyed that we were not all in a room together. Mama, Lasse, Karin and I were in one room, but Papa was somewhere else. I had missed Papa so much and I wanted to be with him, but he never seemed to be around. I asked Mama why we couldn't be with him more and she said we must be patient as he was still suffering from his time in the camps. I asked Mama where he had been and what the Japanese had done to him, but she said he preferred not to talk about it. I asked if she had seen the scars on his back and her eyes welled up with tears as she nodded.

For the first time that evening I went to bed in the pyjamas the Red Cross had given me. It was so warm and I fell asleep straightaway. However, I woke up in the early hours of the morning soaked in sweat, took them off and threw them on the floor. Mama woke and asked what I was doing. I told her that the pyjamas were as stupid as the brown shoes and I wouldn't wear any of them again. Mama laughed and told me I would soon be eating my words. 'Get some sleep, Lisemor. Tomorrow we fly to Rangoon.'

I had never been on an aeroplane before. We walked onto the tarmac at Singapore airport and were ushered towards a huge green military plane. On board, we sat on cold corrugated iron benches and were given cotton wool for our ears. I was a little frightened when the plane took off and it was very noisy. A man told us we would land at Rangoon then fly on to London. I knew from my old geography lessons that London wasn't too far from Norway; now I was getting really excited.

257

We landed twice for fuel stops and slept over in big army barracks somewhere, where we met British and US airmen who gave us sweets and joked with us. They were all very happy and, like us, they were excited about going home. Some of them had been fighting the war for nearly five years, and they told me that many of their friends had been killed. It was all very sad and I felt sorry for them. Some of the men were sick and lay on stretchers in the barracks. Some had arms and legs missing.

We were in Rangoon for nearly a month, waiting for a flight to London. We slept in open dormitories with screens between each family. It reminded me of Bangkong Camp, except we were fed well, had a bed each and had lots of fun. We were given board games to play and books and even an old gramophone with some records. Mama's favourite was 'Indian Love Call' by Jeanette MacDonald; I recall a man by the name of Nelson Eddy singing along with her. We were looked after well and went out with the American and Australian soldiers in Jeeps. We went swimming in lakes and rivers and drove around the countryside on the old Burma Road. We took trips to the seaside and ate sandwiches on the beach. In the month we were in Rangoon, Mama's health improved dramatically. It was Papa I was worried about now. I had expected more from him. I was aware of what a terrible time he had had in the camps, but so had everyone else, and I just wanted to sit with him and talk and play like we used to in Surabaya before the Japanese took us away. He seemed to almost distance himself from his children, and from Mama, too, preferring to spend his time playing cards with some of the soldiers or locking himself in a room with several books.

A message came through to the barracks that the aircraft destined to take us to London had been sabotaged and it would take a month to repair. A man in a smart uniform with a strange moustache that looked like handlebars told us we would be travelling to England by ship.

The ship was called *Llangibby Castle* and it was a troop ship. As we boarded, I noticed happy smiling troops everywhere. They hung over the side, waving at the people on the quayside, and the mothers with children settled in the officers' quarters. We had bunk beds with a little bathroom, and once again we had pillows and soft, nice-smelling blankets. Papa didn't sleep with us in our cabin. Uncle Axel had a small cabin with Aunt Marianne. When I asked Mama about this, she explained that it was only because Uncle Axel was a very important man that he shared a cabin with his wife.

We were on the ship to Southampton for a month, and now we had a new problem. Now that Lasse had been well fed for many weeks he had discovered he could run, and while it was nice to see him run, the deck of a ship wasn't the ideal running track. Everyone was afraid he would fall over the side and we were each given an hour or two every day to watch over him; everyone, that is, except Papa, who spent most of his time below deck.

There were thousands of troops on board; they slept wherever there was space and, where there wasn't space, they strung up hammocks and slept above their friends. There were several hundred civilians on board, too, and around fifty nurses to tend the wounded.

The first half of our passage was pleasant enough, though I ached to be back home in Norway. There was a big restaurant on the ship and eventually our stomachs went back to the way they had once been and we could eat normally. It was nice weather and I enjoyed the sea air and gazing out onto the calm seas and oceans we sailed.

In late November, as we were heading to Ceylon (Sri Lanka), the weather changed. At first it was just a gentle breeze coming off the sea, but soon after I noticed the ship swaying from side to side. The size of the waves increased each hour, as did the power of the wind, and the captain ordered everyone away from the outside decks. We sat on our beds, watching the sea from the small porthole in our cabin as the rain and spray from the sea lashed against it. Before long everyone, including Lasse, was being sick, and even if we closed our eyes and didn't watch the sea, it made no difference.

It got worse as the days passed. The storm was terrifying. I even believed that the ship would simply break in two. It would lurch forward deep into the ocean and then rise up high before crashing back down into the sea with a big bang. It went on hour after hour, day after day, getting worse all the time. People were crying and I recall the look on their faces. Some were worried, and I remember thinking that, after all we had been through, it wasn't right that our ship wasn't going to make it. After several days, the captain informed us we would be heading into Madras for some essential repairs.

At last, as we limped into the port of Madras, the wind died down a little and the rain stopped.

CHAPTER 33

A Norwegian Friend

When we berthed in Madras, the captain came to see us in our cabin. He said there was a Norwegian tanker in the harbour and wondered if we wanted to say hello to the captain. He said he thought it might be nice to speak with some of our fellow countrymen as we were the only Norwegians on board. I was so excited at the thought of going onto another ship and pleaded with Mama to let us go. Mama was not so sure. She said it didn't feel right to bother the busy captain. Our captain replied, 'Not at all, I've spoken to him and he says he would be delighted to speak with you all.'

'And Papa, too?' I asked.

Mama looked at me. 'You think Papa would come?'

We all went. Papa, too.

It was the biggest ship I had ever seen and we were all so excited as we boarded, even though Mama had dressed me up and made me wear those horrible brown shoes. She told me that we would be back in Norway soon and I must start getting used to the cold and wearing real shoes. The deck was huge, as big as the *kampong* back in Surabaya, but there were no passengers. We were taken to the captain's quarters and he introduced himself as Captain Anton. A table was set with sandwiches and beautiful cakes and coffee and we all sat down. Mama and Papa started talking to Captain Anton and I didn't understand a single word they were saying. They were speaking in Norwegian. I looked at Karin and she shrugged her shoulders.

There was a small Norwegian flag in the middle of the table and a picture of a very dignified-looking man on the wall behind Captain Anton.

'Who is that?' I asked Mama, pointing to the picture of the man.

Mama turned around and smiled. 'That is King Haakon VII, Lisemor. That is the King of Norway . . . our King.'

We stayed for an hour or two with Captain Anton and the one overriding memory of that visit was of Papa smiling almost continuously. At last, I thought to myself, he is back with us. He is acting just like the Papa I remember; perhaps he will stay in our cabin tonight?

As we said our goodbyes to Captain Anton, we all agreed to meet up in Norway.

When we got back on board *Llangibby Castle*, I asked Papa to come to our cabin. He shook his head. 'I'll stay down below,' he said. 'All my things are downstairs. It's better that way.' I noticed his smile had gone.

The weather was getting colder and Mama kept telling me I had better get used to it. I persevered with wearing my brown shoes and even started wearing my pyjamas. By now I was concerned about how cold it would be in Norway and I began to prepare my body for the climate of my home country.

Sometimes I stood out on deck for hours in just a thin dress as the weather got colder. I asked Mama each night how cold it would be in Norway and she asked me if I remembered the holiday we had had there just before the war. I remembered bits of the holiday and I remembered the snow and how cold it was on my hands.

It was time to start planning.

Not far from where Papa slept was the galley, where the men prepared all the food. In an open room next to the galley was a huge freezer full of frozen meat. I pulled a crate into the freezer area and sat down.

At first I could stand the cold for no more than a few minutes, but, as each day passed, I counted longer and longer. My body was getting used to the cold; it was working. I'd counted to nearly six hundred one morning when one of the men from the galley disturbed me.

'What on earth are you doing in here?' he asked.

I explained what Mama had said and told him I was getting used to the cold. He laughed, told me not to let him catch me in there again and said I was lucky I hadn't caught pneumonia . . . whatever that was.

*

In the Arabian Sea, just before the Gulf of Aden, we experienced a cyclone. The ship was thrown around like a leaf and the captain ordered us up on deck with safety vests in order to be close to the lifeboats. I recall walking up on deck and noticing one of the women missionaries standing by the open door of her cabin ironing a dress. Unbelievably she was singing. Mama thought she had gone crazy and asked her what she was doing.

She replied to Mama that if she was going to meet her Saviour, she was going to look her best. A little later I spotted her on deck in a beautiful pale-yellow silk dress. After a minute she was soaked to the skin. Just then I noticed a look of panic on Mama's face.

'What is it, Mama?' I asked.

'Karin,' she said. 'Where is Karin?'

We looked around, but Karin was nowhere to be seen. Other people began to take notice of the state Mama was in, and some even looked over the side into the rough, swollen sea. No, I thought, please let her be safe, please . . . not in the sea.

We found Karin tucked up in bed in the cabin. She had heard someone say the ship was going to sink as we made our way to the lifeboats and said that, if that was going to happen, she would rather go down tucked up in her warm bed wearing her nice fluffy pyjamas.

We didn't sink and the storm passed. The lady in the yellow silk dress said it wasn't our day to go and greet the Lord.

We were now in the Suez Canal and the ship was travelling very slowly, trying to avoid the damaged ships and boats that had been blown up and sunk during the war. We took many days to get through the Suez Canal and at night we would stop because it was too dangerous to sail then.

It was in the Suez Canal where it really started to get cold. We dragged big woollen blankets up on deck just to keep warm. In Suez, the Red Cross and RAPWI (Repatriation of Allied Prisoners of War and Internees) organization were waiting with winter clothes for everyone. We went ashore at Suez and had tea and sandwiches. The Red Cross gave us all a huge bag filled with shoes, clothes, hats and scarves, everything we would need in Norway. The Red Cross ladies were lovely, always smiling in their grey uniforms with a red cross.

We reached the Mediterranean Sea by mid-December and by now it was freezing cold. The men on the ship were playing a deadly game called minesweeping. They had huge bamboo poles and hung over the side of the ship, prepared to push mines away from the sides. The men said the mines were left over from the war and that if one of them touched the side of the ship, it would explode and sink us. The men were very serious and sombre, but we children enjoyed the game we called 'hunt the hedgehog'. The men would sit us all at the front of the ship and tell us to look for hedgehogs. I was very scared at this point because the thick fog that wrapped around the ship made it impossible to see anything and the foghorns sounded every few minutes. As we sailed further north, it was too cold and windy for the children to be up on deck so we returned below. The fog lingered for many days. We crossed our fingers and hoped that the men had good eyesight. We were getting impatient, too, because we had hoped to be home for Christmas. Even Papa seemed a little happier now, especially when the nurses were around. Mama often argued with Papa, and one day I recall Aunt Marianne being angry at him, telling him off and saying he had to spend more time with his family.

We had some great news just before Christmas. Mama had a telegram from Norway. Our grandparents were well and looking forward to seeing us, but there was even better news: Uncle Wilhelm had survived the concentration camps in Germany. Everyone thought that Mama's brother must have died as no one had heard anything about him since his capture at the beginning of the war. The telegram went on to say that he was very ill, but they expected him to make a full recovery. Grandad and Grandma said not to worry about Christmas if we weren't back in time. They had lots of gifts for us, and a Christmas tree, but they would wait and we would have our very own special Christmas Day when we arrived.

CHAPTER 34

A Very Special Christmas Present

❧❧❧

We spent Christmas 1945 at sea; the galley provided dinner. It was a bright sunny day but very cold, and after breakfast I went to try and find Papa to wish him a happy Christmas.

As I climbed down some stairs a nice young Englishman wished me a merry Christmas.

'What did Santa bring you?' he asked.

I shrugged my shoulders. 'Nothing,' I said. I hadn't thought about presents as it had been so long since I had received one.

'No presents?' he exclaimed. 'Just you wait there a minute. Little girls shouldn't be without presents on Christmas morning.' Before I could answer he had disappeared. I sat down on the step and waited.

He returned after just a few minutes with his hands hidden behind his back.

He told me to close my eyes, which I did, and I felt him place something in my hands. When I opened them I stared down at a beautiful negro doll dressed in a black silk dress with a red lining. The dress had a wide split and the doll had a white fur cape stitched around her shoulders. The material of the dress was so soft to the touch, and the doll's face was so pretty with bright red painted lips. I couldn't speak, even to thank him; I was so shocked with what he had done. Before I had time to regain my composure and thank him, he placed an orange in my other hand, wished me a happy Christmas again and then he was gone.

I ran back up to Mama's cabin to tell her what had happened and to show her my Christmas present. I gave Karin my orange so she would have something, too; thankfully Lasse was still sleeping. Mama caught me looking at Lasse and told me not to worry about my brother.

'There will be plenty of presents for Lasse when we get back to Norway,' she said.

I looked high and low for the nice Englishman to thank him for the presents, but I never saw him again.

The captain and his crew made Christmas Day 1945 a day to remember. Mama said the men in the galley must have worked all night and we sat down to a real feast. Someone had even taken the time to make a menu, so that we could look forward to what was coming. We sat at a large decorated table with candles and started with some cakes with vanilla sauce. I was determined to try everything on the menu, but Mama told me to be careful. Someone announced later that day that we had left Gibraltar behind and that it was full speed ahead towards the English

Channel. He said the weather was good and in four days we would be docking in Southampton.

We berthed in Southampton on 29 December. It was so terribly cold, dark and foggy, but there were hundreds of people on the quay to greet us. A band played and flags and bunting hung everywhere. It was very emotional and I remember thinking about all the unfortunate people who hadn't made it back. I wondered where Pieter was and Mrs Antje and Kitty, too.

We had a very emotional farewell with Aunt Marianne and Uncle Axel, with kisses and tears. We promised to meet up with them very soon, then they were picked up by a car from their embassy and travelled back to Sweden the next day. So did our Dutch friends.

We were met by a man from the Norwegian consulate and he gave us train tickets to London, where we stayed in Norway House on Shaftesbury Avenue.

We had two rooms at the hotel. I stayed with Karin, and Lasse was with Mama and Papa. It was very frustrating as we seemed to linger there for days. The lady in the hotel explained that there were no offices open during the holidays and we just had to wait, as the Norwegian authorities insisted that our vaccinations had to be complete and all of the paperwork correct. It's stupid, I thought. We are Norwegian; why don't they allow us to come home?

Papa complained a lot and questioned why the Dutch, Danish and Swedish people had been sent home in less than twenty-four hours.

We stayed two weeks in London and spent our time sightseeing. I remember seeing Buckingham Palace, Big Ben and 10 Downing Street, but not much else. The one thing I do remember was the horrible smog that seemed to linger in the London air the whole day. Mama wouldn't go out as she said it was very dangerous, but Papa and I went out quite often. I hoped our little excursions, just the two of us, might make him feel like part of the family and that perhaps he would grow to like us all again.

Eventually Mama and Papa got a phone call from the Norwegian consulate saying that the paperwork was complete and ready for signing. We were sent to a big house for the day, belonging to a sweet old lady, as Mama and Papa went to the offices on the other side of London. The next day we were sent for our vaccinations and I remember Lasse screaming a lot. That evening we were given train tickets to Newcastle upon Tyne. A little while after, Papa announced he would not be coming with us. He had managed to get a job and would be staying in London for the foreseeable future. Mama explained that it was good news as it meant he would be sending us money every month and we were lucky because not many men had jobs as so many factories and offices had been destroyed.

I don't recall much about the train journey to Newcastle, other than that it was freezing cold and I kept wondering why Papa had remained in London. Surely there were jobs in Norway?

In Newcastle upon Tyne we boarded the ship *Astrea* and the journey to Bergen took three days. The North Sea was the most horrible place in the world: freezing cold with higher waves than I could remember seeing before, and snowflakes for the first time.

I stayed in my bed for most of the journey and felt sick all the way. Mama received telegrams from Grandad and I recall she looked so happy. The weather in Bergen was also appalling. It was wet and grey, but no one seemed to care. As the ship edged into the quayside, Mama reminded us all about Grandma's big house, her staircase, the patisserie 'Reimers' and the shops. Karin asked her about the cakes from the bakery and Mama promised we'd go soon.

We were looking forward to our Christmas Day that Grandma and Grandad had promised. At last our family would be together again.

We were out on the deck now and itching to get off the ship. Karin and I held our tatty rucksacks and Mama sat patiently on the lifebelt crates. The quayside was full and amazingly I spotted someone I vaguely remembered. I called Mama over and she walked carefully to the rails. It was Aunty Elsa, she announced, and standing next to her were Grandma and Grandad. As they lowered the huge gangway, some people rushed to get off and others ran from the quayside up onto the ship. It was quite frightening and very chaotic, with lots of shouting, and I was pleased that we had to stay on board to get clearance. As we sat waiting on some crates, we were surrounded by photographers and reporters from newspapers, who asked us many questions. Mama cried tears of joy when eventually Aunt Elsa and Grandad and Grandma found us. Everyone made a fuss of Lasse as they had never seen him. Mama looked on smiling and I sincerely believed that now we were back home in Norway, life would return to normal. Papa would be home soon . . . I just knew it.

Afterword

Adolf Hitler, the Nazis and the Holocaust are well documented, and rightly so. Children learn about the terrible crimes committed in the name of one man and one nation, but less is known about the hell that millions of soldiers, sailors, civilians, women and children experienced in the Far East at the hands of the Japanese. At times it's almost as if it has been conveniently swept away. American attitudes towards Japanese war crimes changed markedly following the 1997 publication of Iris Chang's *The Rape of Nanking*. The moving testament to the Chinese victims in the attack on Nanking in 1937 graphically detailed the horror and scale of the crime and indicted the Japanese government and people for their collective amnesia about their atrocious conduct. Everybody in Europe has heard about the Nuremberg War Trials, but how many of us know about the Tokyo War Crimes Tribunal?

Allied nations held war crimes trials throughout Asia and the Pacific. The Americans, British, Australians, Dutch, French,

Filipinos and Chinese held trials at forty-nine locations between October 1945 and April 1946. The British prosecuted numerous Japanese for war crimes in South-East Asia, including those involved in the construction of the Thai-Burma railway of death, immortalized in *The Bridge Over the River Kwai*. The Batavia War Crimes Tribunal was conducted by Dutch authorities in February 1948. In one case this tribunal tried twelve Japanese soldiers for the forced prostitution of Dutch women held in internment camps in Semarang, Java in 1943. For me, this crime was very close to home. Incredibly, however, the Japanese government decided to parole all of those imprisoned by 1956 and the Foreign Ministry released them unconditionally in April 1958. They hadn't even served fifteen years.

A convicted Class A war criminal, who was a senior diplomat and foreign minister during the war years, regained the foreign minister portfolio in 1953. How could this have been allowed to happen? When confronted, the Japanese government insisted that these issues had been settled by stipulations of the peace treaty signed in San Francisco in September 1951. Nothing more needed to be said on the matter, they claimed. Not only did the Japanese authorities refuse to acknowledge any wartime responsibility, but several conservative politicians and senior bureaucrats went so far as to publicly denounce the accusations as groundless historical revisionism and Japan bashing.

Germany publicly accepted responsibility for the evils perpetrated by the Nazi regime and educated future generations by discussing its sordid Nazi history in school textbooks and classes. Germany apologized to various European nations and to Israel. Conversely, Japan rejected responsibility, downplayed the historical evidence of aggression and atrocity in its schools and apologized to no one. Even worse, ultra-conservative Japanese commentators insisted the war crimes, if they happened at all, were exaggerated to embarrass the Japanese people. I can assure you that they were certainly not exaggerated. If anything, this book has downplayed the ferocity and barbaric actions of the Japanese. My mother was always at pains to point out to me that we children were shielded from the worst of it.

Of course we cannot continue to cast blame on a generation that knew nothing about the crimes of their fathers and grand-fathers.

I want closure on my times in the camps, and by writing this book I feel I have taken a huge step towards that. I want to be able to look a Japanese person in the eye and feel respect and not look upon him or her with fear and loathing. I want to be able to hug a Japanese person comfortably, without the hairs on the back of my neck standing to attention and a cold sweat covering my body. I do.

I wish I could go back in time and confront my tormentors. I wish I could say to them, 'Do you realize that your barbaric actions, your murder, rape and torture, will never be forgotten? How would you feel if I tell you that your children, grand-children and great-grandchildren will be looked upon with revulsion by certain members of society?' Would it have made a difference to the nation that knew no wrong?

I want Japan to say sorry in a symbolic gesture that is both sincere and meaningful, but I doubt that this will happen in my lifetime. Unfortunately 'forgiveness' is not in my vocabulary as far as the Japanese are concerned and therefore maybe my closure will never be complete.

Lasse was still a little young to think about life after the war – life in our home country of Norway – but for Karin, and me especially, we thought that life would return to normal and everything would be perfect. Although we didn't have the tropical warm weather of Java in Norway, I envisaged that we would be together as a family once again, experience those carefree days having fun, where we ate what we wanted when we wanted, visited restaurants when we liked and had sufficient money for the everyday essentials of life, with a few luxuries on top. I didn't expect servants or trips out to open-air swimming pools and days at the beach, but I had hoped and dreamed often of coming back to our lovely home country while we sat starving on the blue door. I prayed to a God I didn't believe in that we would manage to survive the hell we were in and, once back home, that we would recreate the same family atmosphere I remembered before the Japanese took over our lives. However, it wasn't to be.

I remember Papa being very distant on the journey home to Europe and I felt a great uneasiness, as I didn't really know what was going on between the grown-ups. They both looked sullen and bored, and we resented the fact that our handsome father, who had survived untold hardships, just like most of us, could not enjoy being with his stricken family. Things came to a head when he suddenly announced that he would stay behind and apply for a job in London. Our family was already divided before we came home.

It seemed we had come home to incredibly difficult times. Papa was still in London and had not been able to send us any of his wages. Norway in the post-war years ran on rationing cards and the shelves of the shops were almost empty. Our grandparents worked hard to keep our sorry 'refugee family' in food, clothing and other necessities, but I recall an almost permanent sad, strained atmosphere in the house.

Mama was very irritable, which resulted in many cross words. She was very sick with rheumatism and in almost permanent discomfort. Her legs swelled up after just a short walk and it made her very depressed. Sometimes she was in such pain that it was only possible to walk down the stairs backwards. It was a sorry sight. I felt so sure that she would be well again after we had left the Japanese concentration camps, but it seemed the damage inflicted on her during those times was too severe for her body to repair. Mama did not like having to rely on our grandparents for anything other than the food they provided, and when we did get a little money from Papa it was very carefully managed. There were some days when she could not make it out of the house to go shopping because of her health, and other days when she was fit enough but had no money. Fortunately, we had a kind family in Oslo: Grandma's siblings. They sent parcels, often with cast-off clothes that Mama and Grandma altered so they would fit us. We thought we looked great, and not at all different from our schoolmates.

Mama was a very proud lady; before the war she had wanted for nothing and money was no object. We were always dressed immaculately and presented well whenever we left the house, even if it was just to play. Now she was sending us out in cast-off clothes and it hurt her. We walked past clothes shops with nice things in the window, but Mama just took our hands and guided us away. She smiled bravely and said to us, 'Walk quickly, look happy and nobody will notice anything.' I remember too well that we always were told to 'pull ourselves together' whenever we felt ill or depressed.

There was nothing called emergency assistance in those days. No one cared when we felt anxious or traumatized. I so wanted Papa to come home to Norway and live with us. Even when he did come to Norway for a weekend, he always stayed with his parents, not with us. They explained that there was no room for him in our house. Even when I offered to sleep on the floor he still stayed at his mother's. Papa told me he was working as an auditor for a company called Northraship and that there were no jobs for him in Norway. I remember being very frustrated; surely there were jobs in Norway, I thought to myself.

Mama could not work and complained about how little Papa was sending from London. However, she protected him, too, telling us that the cost of living was very high there and that he paid a lot of money each week just for a tiny bedsit. I was sad thinking of poor Papa in a small bedsit all on his own.

Mama went laboriously to and from physicians and insurance offices to try and get some financial support, but it was nigh on impossible. She felt we deserved some help, some sort of compensation for everything we had been through at the hands of the Japs in the camps. She said she would love to be able to work, but the Japanese had almost killed her. They should at least have to pay something to help stricken people like us survive. Japan was not at all interested in paying any form of compensation or assistance. They had done nothing wrong, they said – it was our war!

In desperation Mama even contacted the Dutch Foreign Ministry; perhaps they would be able to talk the Japs into paying out some compensation. They told Mama they could not help us as we had Norwegian passports. Mama remarked, 'We have fallen between two stools.' She was desperate and I felt for her. At times she looked even more unhappy than when she had sat on the blue door. We all expected that life would be just perfect when we returned to Norway, but now the harsh reality had well and truly set in. Finally, in the middle of 1947, I saw her smiling one day. A letter had arrived from the National Insurance.

We were to receive a payment of kr.10.68 (one pound sterling) per day for one adult with three children. It appeared that this was the biggest amount the office would pay out. They had assessed the Grønn-Nielsen family 100 per cent damaged as a result of our years at the hands of the Japanese. Mama's health never improved and she was never able to work again.

Incredibly, it wasn't until the beginning of 1970 that she was awarded an invalid war pension in her own right.

We started Norwegian schooling, a proper school, but memories of my last ill-fated lesson in the Bangkong Monastery were never far away. I was placed into the fourth grade of Nygård School. I was a year older than the others as I was behind with my schooling, not to mention the Norwegian language. Miss Ljustvedt and thirty-one of my classmates did the best they could to help me settle in. It was a great time, although I did not understand much of what was going on. My Norwegian was still very bad, despite the endeavours of Mama and my grandparents at home, who by now were only speaking in Norwegian. To me and Karin it was simply a foreign language, but gradually we picked it up.

I had difficulties adapting to the necessary discipline that Miss Ljustvedt had built up in the years the class had been together, and nor could I get used to the timing of the class and constantly having to keep an eye on the clock. For nearly three years we hadn't even seen a clock or a watch. We had gauged the time by the sun as it rose in the morning and set at night, or from the regular *tenkos* in the mornings.

Every day we were given cod liver oil, milk and 'Swedish soup'. Karin and I could hardly control our excitement as we pushed our way to the front of the queue, more than a little worried that the girls at the back might lose out. Food still had that effect on us. Our classmates would look on wondering what all the fuss was about. 'It's only a little foul-tasting food,' they would say.

Afterword

Back at home, Mama seemed to be in a constant state of frustration. Everything got her down: the school system, the language problem, finance and, of course, her health; everything, even everyday life. For me and Karin it wasn't so bad. School was an exciting and challenging environment and we made lots of good friends.

I loved gymnastics and was advised one day that I had been accepted into Bergen Turnforening (Gymnastics Academy). I was absolutely ecstatic and couldn't wait to start. I went each week with my friend Aud, taking the short walk through Bergen. One afternoon I heard a deep rumbling noise behind me. I looked back and, to my horror, saw a large number of military trucks covered with green tarpaulins. I recoiled into the nearest doorway.

I was trembling and shaking and Aud asked me over and over again what was wrong. I don't know how long I cowered in that doorway, perhaps only a few minutes, but in my head I was back in the camps again, awaiting the transport that took us from one hellhole to another. The trucks were parked along the sidewalk and were full of soldiers in green uniforms. They stood close together at the back of the truck. I did not understand anything. My heart pounded and my stomach churned with fear. I remember breathing heavily and the sweat stood out on my brow. I wanted to cover my eyes, but was somehow drawn to look up. I looked into the eyes of the soldiers and breathed a sigh of relief that they were not the eyes of the Japs. I looked some more; the soldiers did not have rifles with bayonets attached.

My breathing slowed as Aud reassured me that everything was fine. I tried hard to compose myself and looked at the reaction of the Norwegian people going about their normal daily business. They walked past the trucks, hardly giving them a second look. I stayed in the doorway until the trucks had passed. Only then did I continue on my way. Mama later explained that they were German soldiers who had been taken prisoner after the war. They were on their way home to Germany. The Germans had occupied Norway for five terrible years, she said. I recalled those German soldiers in the trucks. They looked well; they had been fed and had warm clothes; they all wore a thick woolly hat; some of them were even laughing and joking. There had been no laughing and joking in the concentration camps in Java. It did not look like they had been suffering at all.

The war was uppermost in our thoughts and discussions at home. At school we were taught all about it. Uncle Wilhelm told us of the awful years he'd spent in German concentration camps and how it was a miracle that he'd survived. He had been rescued by the Swedish 'white buses' that came to the concentration camps and brought home the survivors. As I talked with Uncle Wilhelm and heard of his terrible ordeal at the hands of the Germans, I remembered the German soldiers in the trucks. There was no reason to feel sorry for the soldiers aboard those trucks. No one had yelled at them or beat them and no one had stabbed them with bayonets.

One of the most difficult things to get used to was the weather. It was simply awful; it was always cold and it rained almost constantly. Nevertheless we still learned to enjoy life in Norway. We got food every day and slept in clean beds with pillows and duvets. Old habits took time to overcome, however. I still emptied shoes, boots and slippers before I put them on, just in case there was a scorpion inside. Although our relationship with our grandparents was very good, they had difficulties accepting our strange behaviour. I suppose we were quite unruly and ill-disciplined in their eyes, but we were just making the most of the freedom that had been denied us for so long.

We were anxious, did not like sudden, sharp noises, or angry, high-pitched reprimands. As the months and years passed, I realized that many of our problems stemmed from our years in captivity. In particular, Karin and Lasse felt great insecurity when Mama was not close by. My biggest problem was the night-mares that haunted me almost every night. I was always running – running and hiding – and when the people who were chasing me eventually found me, as they inevitably did, they wore the uniform of the Imperial Japanese Army, their teeth were yellow and broken, stained brown and black, and they screamed and shouted at me as I slept. I hid under benches and in crates and screwed my eyes tight shut in the forlorn hope that, if I couldn't see them, they wouldn't see me. They jabbed at me with their bayonets, kicked out at me with their hard leather boots and dragged me out by my hair. And then I would wake in a cold sweat, shivering with fear. The nightmares always woke me and I would search for Mama. Often she would not be in her bedroom and I would find her in the drawing room.

I have a clear picture, a vision of Mama sitting in front of the window, dissolved in tears. I can still picture her against that window, the rain pounding against the glass pane. The rain made long uneven patterns down the windowpane, and Mama was silhouetted against the gleaming streetlights outside. In the shadows it gave the impression that her whole face and hair was crying. I would gently ask what it was that was making her so upset, but she never answered.

I could not help pilfering food. I discovered that Grandma had a secret stock of food in her own little cabinet. For me it was like an Aladdin's cave. She had a small stock of bread, butter and delicious meats, and she also had a beautiful block of dairy butter. I was always so hungry and the butter was so delicious, I ate it with a small spoon. Of course, Grandma soon found out about my incursion of her supplies and scolded me many times, telling me she had diabetes and the food was very important to her. She told Mama and Mama scolded me, saying there was nothing worse than stealing from the very people who were feeding you. I hung my head in shame and promised I would not do it again. But of course I couldn't help myself. I knew it was wrong, but I was always overcome with the feeling that if I didn't take something it would disappear forever. I also convinced myself that no one would notice the small portions I took. Grandma eventually put a padlock on the cupboard door, but even then I thought about ways in which I could force the lock.

Grandma was rarely in a good mood. The food and clothes coupons hardly sufficed for her extended family. Some week-ends we travelled to Askøy out in the country, where Grandad rented a small cottage with a dental surgery for the community. His patients were farmers and paid him with fresh produce like chickens, eggs, fish and meat. Some were budding painters and could only offer him their pictures. There are now pictures on the family walls from some who are well-known painters today. We used to spend happy summer holidays there with our lovely cousins. Grandad, a sweet-natured, kind man, loved it out there in Askøy, especially when his grandchildren ran around, playing, swimming and generally enjoying themselves.

We had some good, carefree times with Papa's family, too – Grandad Gabriel, who was a merchant ship's captain, and Grandma Alma. Sadly, they were divorced. Gabriel lived with his much younger wife, 'Mommen', and their two lovely daughters Mossa and Annemor, in Helleveien, Bergen, while Alma lived alone in the centre of Bergen. Alma and Gabriel's three sons, Carlos, Jørgen and Papa Daniel were born in Las Palmas, Spain, where they had a house. So, as a whole, we ended up with a nice extended family Grønn-Nielsen, even if our Papa was mostly absent.

It was as though the horrors of the camps had never happened.

Every two or three weeks a burly, jolly man came to the house, carrying big ice blocks on his back to the kitchen below stairs, where we had a 'fridge larder'. Eggs lying in big pots with a mixture of foul smelly brine to keep them fresh longer, were also part of our food storage. Fish was kept salted in drums, and small containers of fresh milk were also stored in the icebox.

We had the odd happy days of baking when flour and other necessary ingredients could be obtained. Once a month it was laundry day in the basement with our maid, Lina, helping out. Big, black drums were filled with clothes, bleach and soapy water and left to soak overnight, then it was boiled on black coal-burning stoves. It was an enormous task, and it took days to finish the mangling and ironing, but we used to enjoy these special days, away from the drabness of everyday life and hours of studying the Norwegian language. Once a week our 'sweet coupon' could be spent; all the kids would queue outside the local shop, hoping for a bar of chocolate, if it was available.

Captain Anton contacted us when he returned to Lillehammer. It was so nice to hear from him again. I had been lucky enough to be invited to Oslo for the summer holidays with the family and would be living with Aunt Lully and Uncle Jørgen Lorentzen in Hankø. Karin was going to Lillehammer to be pampered by Captain Anton and his family. Everyone was looking forward to it, especially Mama, who said she would be glad of the rest, but the joy was short-lived.

Karin and I were still so uncertain, so scared to be parted from Mama, that we suffered from homesickness the minute we left her. We had panic attacks, were very tearful and sometimes got angry with our friends who were giving us such a nice time. I think I fared better than Karin in Lillehammer; she was there for nearly three months and cried herself to sleep almost every night. Aunt Lully and Uncle Jørgen kept telling me that I had to stay for the sake of Mama, who was enjoying the rest and recovering well, so I persevered. When I returned home I fully expected Mama to be well again, but she wasn't; she was the same sorry specimen we had left behind. It was as if her body was permanently broken, twisted and contorted in agony at the slightest effort. Poor Mama.

In the autumn of 1947 we received some good news: Mama had been given a place at the Rheumatism Hospital in Oslo. However, our joy was about to be shattered. Grandma decided that she could not manage three children alone for the many weeks Mama would be away, so poor Lasse would have to go into an orphanage just outside Oslo. I was horrified and protested angrily that I could take care of him, as I had always done in the camps. Grandma reminded me about school and lessons, which had to take priority. She explained that it would only be for a few weeks and that was that. I didn't have any say in the matter. I was devastated at the thought of being separated from Lasse, but more so at the fact that he wouldn't be with anyone he knew.

Without anybody knowing, I wrote a letter to Aunt Marianne in Stockholm and asked her if she could look after Lasse while Mama was in hospital. Unfortunately, she had recently started a translation agency and could not help us. I sent a letter to Papa in London, too, but he couldn't take any time off work, though he did say that he would be home in a few weeks. It was a terribly disturbing and unhappy time for Lasse; he was barely five years old. They had a big problem with him at the orphanage as he constantly tried to escape. On one occasion he ran into a large plate-glass window, which smashed into a hundred pieces. Poor Lasse was cut to shreds and had to be taken to hospital, where he was stitched up.

Thankfully Mama was only away one month and soon returned to Bergen. She collected Lasse on the way home and I told her about Papa's letter and how he would be home soon. It was wonderful to be with her again and I had renewed hope that the Grønn-Nielsen family would soon be together. Even Mama seemed a little different, happier with life in general. She had benefited from her stay in hospital and did not need to go backwards down the stairs any more.

Life was back to normal and I remembered happy times. We were all together: Grandma, Grandad, Mama, Lasse, Karin and me. The only person missing was Papa. I could hardly contain my excitement when Mama said she had had a letter from him and he was due home at the weekend. It won't be long now, I thought: not long before we are all together in our own house, just like in Java. But when he came home, he asked Mama for a divorce. It was an enormous shock for me; my dream had been destroyed. I feared that we would not have any money to buy food and clothes, and that we would never see him again. I was in despair, totally inconsolable. How could he do this to us? He admitted he had met a Norwegian secretary in his office in London and explained quite casually that he now lived with her.

I could not understand how he could abandon Mama, who was so sick, and leave her all alone to take care of three children. Papa tried to placate me; he said he would continue to send money for food and that he would come to visit as often as he could. It did not go down very well. I felt cheated and abandoned and very angry with him. Was his new secretary more important than his family? I became withdrawn and thought about him a lot. I realized, even at that young age, that he had never really been there for Mama or his family. I was later told that while he was married to Mama he could not leave the ladies alone and that it had made her very unhappy. Even after we had survived the camps, and everyone was so helpless, sick and weak, he was unable to show any real emotion or help us in any way.

On New Year's Eve 1947, Mama was invited to a ball. Uncle Egil Vedeler was to be her escort and we all tried to help her look as beautiful as possible. The never-ending supply of drugs and painkillers she continued to take had made her hair thin and lifeless, but Karin and I arranged it as best we could and took many hours to make her look nice. Her dress was stunning, even though it was a hand-me-down from Grandma's sister. Mama looked beautiful and for once her eyes shone; it was the first time I could recall for a long time. The main problem was finding some nice new shoes. We tried many pairs but her swollen legs and ankles could not cope with them and she winced in pain as she tried each pair on. In the end we touched up her old, comfortable ones with a little paint and convinced her that her long ballgown would hide the bits we couldn't put right.

The party was a success and she even managed a few dances, though her feet were very sore the next day. Some weeks later, an elegant, handsome man came to take Mama to the cinema. She had met him at the New Year's Eve ball. I remember looking at her when he arrived, and I saw in her eyes how happy she was to see him. His name was Bernhard Martin Frønsdal and he became her new husband in July 1949. Papa married Kari Meinich Gran the same year, and they had a daughter, Anne Carolyn, and Mama, our brave mother, had a son, Martin Bernhard.

Mama's health improved slightly as the years went by, but her arthritis and rheumatism never left her. The pains in her legs reminded her almost daily of those terrible times during the war.

Mama died in 1979; Papa died in 1971.

We siblings fought our demons and managed to make our way quite successfully in the world. Poor Lasse suffered the most healthwise; during those early years he had been deprived of essential vitamins and this took its toll. Nevertheless, he became a very good artist and founded his own advertising agency. He was also a very successful designer. Karin qualified as a nurse and a very good one at that. I remember her watching and studying the nurses in the camp at Lampersarie, carrying out their duties under impossible conditions, and I can't help feeling that somehow those angels shaped her destiny. Karin's health suffered, too, as a result of what we had gone through, with conditions such as diabetes. After years living in Spain, the US and the Philippines, she has now returned to Norway and is happily settled in Bergen.

As for me, eventually I went in search of the sun, too. My late teens were spent in Oslo, living in small, gloomy bedsits. After work, eventually as a private secretary, my time was spent in the gymnastics academy.

When friends introduced me to my first husband, I thought that life would surely change for the better. He was a very handsome man who had trained to be a police officer and he subsequently changed career and joined the Norwegian Air Force, becoming a captain.

Two beautiful children later, whom I happily tried to bring up to the best of my ability, all seemed to be just fine. Then life changed as it turned out he could not leave the ladies alone. Just like my father. My health deteriorated and severe depression followed. My sister, who at the time had settled in Spain with her two boys, invited me to stay. She helped me out of some of my misery with endless talks, going back to our years in the camp. Eventually we both applied for – and received – a war pension, after numerous appointments with psychiatrics and psychologists. For me it was still very difficult to come to terms with the awful times my children must have suffered, resulting in constant feelings of guilt.

Eventually, after a very sad divorce, my husband married one of his girlfriends and set up home with his and her children. I found my way back to my sister in Spain, hoping all would turn out well at last, but unfortunately my children were unhappy with the arrangement, and so was I. My mind was in total turmoil and life was unbearable. Then I met a nice young Englishman who worked in Spain. He made me laugh and we enjoyed ourselves, with my children visiting us during the holidays. Life was great, but work possibilities for him were better in the UK, so we settled in Essex and married. I enjoyed my painting courses and worked full time painting and exhibiting.

It turned out I had been quite naive, and to my cost found that life was not all rosy outside our happy home. My Englishman turned out to be a charming small-time crook and stints in prison followed. For twelve years I tried to remain a loving, loyal wife, but when he did the ultimate cruel deed – producing a son by a local girl – my world collapsed again. Even my children, who adored him, could not believe it. With most of my savings gone, I returned to Spain to pick up the pieces again.

My health had suffered in the English weather, so Spain was just what the doctor ordered, and my sister proved to be the right company, too.

'I survived prisoner-of-war camps, and I will survive this, too,' I told my husband, and I rented an apartment and got on with life.

Mama had several visits from other camp survivors during the first few years back in Norway, including her friend the doctor and one of the nurses. I have always believed that they were the ones that kept her alive; there always seemed to be a bed available when Mama needed it the most. They were absolute angels. Some survivors, who sent letters or made phone contact, were so traumatized and weak that they passed away very early. Many did not want to talk about their experience as it was too painful.

I remember one lady who came to see Mama. She was on

her way back to Surabaya to try and retrieve her jewellery from Camp De Wijk and she wondered if Mama wanted her to bring hers as well. She later wrote a letter to Mama telling her that a block of flats had been built on the site. The construction workers must have had a field day, and the ladies had a good laugh.

Sadly, I have had no contact with my friends Pieter and Kitty, nor the lovely Mrs Antje or Jolien. I sincerely hope they made it out alive, as the natives kept on playing their deadly game of throwing hand grenades into the camps. Our Uncle Axel was informed about those atrocities after we arrived at the sanctuary of the Swedish consulate. We were the lucky ones.

In 1993 I travelled back to Indonesia. The people, millions of them, the clinging heat and smells – it was all there. Friends helped me get to the places I wished to see. Unfortunately, the church was the only place I remembered and could get access to. Camp Lampersarie had been turned into army barracks and was off limits, but I got close enough to take snapshots of the surroundings and one of the men's camps, which is now a dilapidated prison. I visited places where I was sure the family had been before the war, and stayed high up in posh hotels. I was proud to be able to look across the town of Semarang, where all the horrors took place, and later Surabaya, my birthplace. I studied the drab *kampong*s with all their filth, and the ugly new high-rise office buildings nearby, knowing that after all my family had gone through, we had survived.

From my two children, Erik and Ellen Hamremoen, I am now the proud grandmother of five: Linn Kristin, Helene, Daniel,

Simen and Aksel. And in August 2011 I became a great-grandmother to a beautiful little boy called Kasper. On the whole my physical health has been good, except for the rheumatoid arthritis I inherited from my mother. I am able to hide my anxiety well. Sadly, the nightmares still come to me occasionally. The pain and heartache of my times in the concentration camps is locked in my subconscious, and I fear it will only be exorcized when I am no longer here. I want to rid myself of my fears, my demons and, of course, my bitterness towards the Japanese, but sadly I can't. I want to, I really do, but I can't.

Life seemed easier after my pilgrimage and my health improved. One day I ran into an old schoolfriend from boarding school in Dale I Sunnfjord, forty-five years after we first met. He was a handsome retired naval officer, recently divorced with two grown-up children, like me. Kristen and I hit it off immediately, and have now been together in Spain for seventeen years. In 1999, Kristen booked a cruise to Hawaii, and we were married in Honolulu.

We visited Pearl Harbor and went onboard the USS *Missouri*, where the peace treaty was signed. The guide told us how General MacArthur treated the Japanese diplomats that day. The six tallest sailors on the ship guarded the deck as they arrived, and he made the short Japs line up with their backs to the Emperor, leaving them there for quite a while. This was in Tokyo Bay.

We travelled there on a sightseeing bus, and when it became known that I had been a prisoner of war under the Japanese, everyone jumped off the bus to have their picture taken with me.

In 2009 we returned to Hawaii for our ten-year wedding anniversary, and went onboard the USS *Missouri* again. It had all started on 7 December 1941, when Japan attacked Pearl Harbor. The Instrument of Surrender was signed on 2 September 1945, and now the circle was complete for me.

Acknowledgements

Thanks to my husband, Kris, who has taken a keen interest in this project by being my secretary.